THRIVING *in* UNCERTAINTY:
Coping with Job Security Pressures & Overcoming the Fear of Redundancy

Patrick E. Okonji

"In the middle of every difficulty lies opportunity."
— Albert Einstein

Contents

Preface 9
Part 1: 11
Understanding Job Security and Redundancy Pressures 11
Chapter 1: Introduction 12
   1.1 The Changing Workplace 12
   1.2. Why This Book Matters 14
   1.3. The Landscape of Job Security 17
   1.4. The Evolving Definition of Job Security 18
   1.5. The Decline of Lifelong Employment 19
   1.6. The Rise of the Gig Economy 20
   1.7. Benefits and Drawbacks of the New Models 21
   1.8. Societal Impacts of the Shift 23
   1.9. Building a New Framework for Job Security 25
   1.10 The Future of Job Security 27
   1.10 The Impact of Redundancy: 28
      1.10.1. Social Consequences 29
      1.10.2. Financial Instability 32
      1.10.3. The Broader Impact on Families 33
   1.11. Recovery and Resilience 35
   1.12. Role of Employers and Society 37
   1.13 Moving Forward 39
Chapter 2: Common Fears Around Job Security 42
   2.1. Common Fears Around Job Security 42
      2.1.1. Fear of Losing Income 43
      2.1.2. Loss of Identity 45
      2.1.3. Fear of the Unknown 47
   2.2. Comparisons and Social Stigma 50

2.3. Strategic Coping Mechanisms and Resilience..................................52

2.4. Conclusion 55

Chapter 3: The Psychological and Emotional Toll..56

3.1. The Psychological and Emotional Toll..56

    3.1.1. Stress and Burnout 58

    3.1.2. Anxiety and Depression 58

    3.1.3. Avoidance and Paralysis 59

3.2. The Role of Leadership in Reducing Stress 64

    3.2.1. Long-Term Implications of Unaddressed Stress 66

    3.2.2. Building Resilience in the Workforce..69

    3.2.3. A Call for Comprehensive Support Systems 71

Part 2: 74

Proactive Strategies for Navigating Job Security Challenges.......................74

Chapter 4: Building Career Resilience: Key Issues and Concerns 75

4.1. Adaptability 75

4.2. Adaptability: The Cornerstone of Resilience 78

4.3. Networking: The Value of Professional Relationships....................79

4.4. Challenges in Networking 79

4.5. The Intersection of Adaptability, Learning, and Networking.........82

4.6. The Role of Organizations in Building Resilient Careers 84

4.7. Building a Resilient Workforce 86

Chapter 5: Creating Multiple Income Streams 89

5.1. Creating Multiple Income Streams: Building Financial Resilience......89

5.2. Developing Side Hustles and Freelance Work 89

5.3. The Flexibility of Freelance Work 90

5.4. Exploring Passive Income Opportunities 91

5.5. Challenges of Passive Income...91

5.6. Entrepreneurial Ventures: Transforming Skills into a Business..........94

5.6.1. The Potential of Entrepreneurship 94

5.6.2. The Challenges of Entrepreneurship 95

5.7. Strategies for Success 96

5.8. Scaling a Business 97

5.8.1. Opportunities in Scaling 97

5.8.2. Challenges of Scaling 98

5.8.3. Strategies for Effective Scaling 99

5.8.4. The Long-Term Vision 100

5.9. Balancing Multiple Income Streams 101

5.9.1. The Benefits and Challenges of Diversification 101

5.9.2. Tools for Effective Management 101

5.9.3. Maintaining Realistic Expectations 102

5.9.4. Leveraging Technology for Income Diversification 103

Chapter 6: Taking Control of Your Finances 106

6.1. Taking Control of Your Finances: A Foundation for Security and Growth 106

6.1.1. Building an Emergency Fund 106

6.1.2. Managing Debt Wisely 107

6.1.3. Living Within Your Means 107

6.1.4. Reducing Financial Stress and Building a Path to Stability 108

6.2. Looking Beyond the Basics 108

6.2.1. Emergency Funds: A Lifeline in Uncertain Times 109

6.2.2. Challenges in Building Emergency Funds 111

6.2.3. Debt Management: Reducing Financial Strain 111

6.2.4. Barriers to Effective Debt Management 113

6.3. Overcoming Challenges to Living Within Means 115

6.4. The Long-Term Benefits of Financial Control 115

6.5. Conclusion 116

Part 3: Coping with Redundancy and Finding Fulfillment 117

Chapter 7: Managing Emotional Fallout 118

7.1. Managing Emotional Fallout: Navigating the Challenges of Redundancy 118

7.2. Acceptance: Acknowledging Feelings Without Judgment 120

7.3. Overcoming the Fear of Vulnerability 122

7.4. Support Systems: The Importance of Connection 123

7.5. Building a Network of Support 126

7.6. Self-Care Practices: Replenishing Energy and Self-Esteem 128

7.7. Rebuilding Confidence Through Self-Care 131

    7.7.1. Balancing Rest and Productivity 131

    7.7.2. Recognizing the Role of Gratitude 134

    7.7.3. Balancing Productivity and Leisure 136

7.8. Finding Fulfillment Beyond Work 136

7.9. Conclusion: Navigating Emotional Recovery with Purpose 139

Chapter 8: Turning Job Loss into Opportunity 140

8.1. Reassessing Your Path: Discovering True Passions 142

8.2. Embracing Change as Growth 143

8.3. Skill Realignment: The Power of Transferable Skills 145

8.4. Skill Realignment: Mapping Strengths to Market Needs 146

8.5. Expanding Career Options Through Transferable Skills 147

    8.5.1. Leveraging Transferable Skills to Build Confidence 148

    8.5.2. Upskilling to Bridge Gaps 148

8.6. Strategic Job Hunting: Crafting a Winning Resume 151

    8.6.1. Optimizing Your LinkedIn Profile 154

    8.6.2. Personalized Job Applications: Quality Over Quantity 157

    8.6.3. Networking for Opportunities 158

    8.6.4. Rebuilding Confidence During the Job Search 158

8.7. Conclusion: Turning Setbacks into Stepping Stones 160

Chapter 9: Living a Fulfilled Life Despite Uncertainty 161

9.1. Redefining Success: Moving Beyond Job Titles 161
9.2. Practicing Gratitude: The Power of the Present Moment................162
9.3. Pursuing Interests: Enriching Life Through Passion.........................163
9.4. Building Connections Through Community Engagement................164
9.5. The Role of Mindset in Fulfillment 166
9.6. Thriving Despite Uncertainty..167
9.7. Conclusion 167

Preface

Many people struggle with anxieties of uncertainty and redundancy as job security and professional stability become more elusive in today's fast-paced society. This book provides readers with a thorough toolset to help them deal with these trying times with resilience and confidence by examining the psychological, emotional, and practical issues related to job instability. The essay offers practical methods for turning obstacles into opportunities by tackling important topics including redefining success, handling emotional repercussions, developing professional resilience, and generating numerous revenue sources.

From establishing financial safeguards like emergency funds and effective debt management to leveraging transferable skills and pursuing fulfilling activities beyond work, this book empowers readers to take control of their lives despite external uncertainties. It emphasizes the importance of acceptance, support systems, and self-care in fostering emotional recovery and offers practical guidance for reassessing career paths, strategic job hunting, and engaging in meaningful community activities.

The book encourages readers to view redundancy as an opportunity to reconnect with their beliefs and passions rather than as a point of termination by redefining career transitions as a path of reinvention, growth, and discovery via the use of flexibility, gratitude, optimism, and proactive planning. It emphasizes the value of human resilience above all else, reminding readers that their value is determined by their individual skills, inner fortitude, and ability to flourish in the face of adversity rather than by their job title. This post offers hope and a path to creating a meaningful and powerful future, regardless of whether you're dealing with unstable employment or looking for ideas for a happy existence.

Part 1:

Understanding Job Security and Redundancy Pressures

Chapter 1: Introduction

1.1 The Changing Workplace

For many professionals, the prospect of job instability looms big in today's rapidly evolving workplace. Job stability frequently seems like an unattainable ideal due to corporate reorganizations, technological automation, and economic downturns. Redundancy anxieties have increased as a result of these changes, making it difficult for employees to adjust and find methods to prosper in the face of uncertainty. There are, unquestionably, difficulties associated with the evolving workplace, but there are also chances for adaptability and creativity.

Over the past ten years, there has been a substantial change in the global labor market. Processes have been optimized by automation and artificial intelligence (AI), which has decreased the requirement for some job kinds while increasing the need for new talents. The environment is further complicated by economic forces of inflation and volatile markets. Furthermore, businesses are embracing smaller, more flexible organizational structures at an increasing rate, which frequently leads to reorganizations and layoffs. Employees are forced by these developments to face the fact that even jobs that were previously secure might become outdated.

Today's increasing automation is one of the biggest causes of job anxieties. Many workers are increasingly skeptical about the value of human labor since robots can now seamlessly, quickly, and accurately complete tasks that formerly needed human effort. Not just low-skilled occupations are being affected by this technological disruption; the legal, medical, and financial sectors are all being affected. Automation increases productivity, but it also makes it more important than ever for workers to upskill in order to compete in a technologically advanced society.

These constraints are made worse by economic downturns, which frequently lead businesses to emphasize cost-cutting strategies like downsizing. For example, the COVID-19 epidemic brought attention to the precarious state of employment across several industries, compelling millions of workers to face their dread of layoffs. Job security thus becomes a major worry for both companies and employees since the effects of such crises persist even after economies recover.

In today's workplace, restructuring has also become commonplace. Businesses frequently reassess their objectives and shift course to satisfy consumer expectations, which can lead to organizational changes that leave workers unsure of their responsibilities. Such disruptions frequently erode trust, productivity, and morale, but they also highlight how crucial flexibility is as a professional skill.

Employees can take proactive measures to manage job instability and develop resilience in spite of these obstacles. In this sense, lifelong learning is a crucial tactic. Professionals may establish themselves as invaluable assets by consistently learning new skills and keeping up with industry developments. Strong professional relationships may lead to new possibilities and serve as a support system during trying times, therefore networking is equally crucial.

Developing an innovative and flexible mentality is another essential component of prospering in the face of uncertainty. Employees might view technology developments and restructuring as chances for progress if they embrace change instead of fighting it. Gaining transferable skills, including communication, problem-solving, and emotional intelligence, may also act as a safety net, allowing employees to change careers or sectors as required. Organizations are essential in reducing concerns about job security. Initiatives for staff assistance, upskilling, and transparent communication may all contribute to the development of stability and trust. Businesses that make investments in their employees not only retain top talent but also boost morale and productivity in general.

Ultimately, it takes both individual and collective effort to overcome the fear of job security. Employees must continue to be proactive, flexible, and receptive to new opportunities in the ever-evolving workplace. Professionals may successfully manage the changing labor market with resilience and confidence if they see uncertainty as a driving force for progress rather than a hindrance. Even if the future is unknown, there is a lot of promise for those who are up for the task.

1.2. Why This Book Matters

Fear of work instability is a very personal one that affects one's sense of identity and self-worth in addition to one's financial security. In a world when our social standing is frequently determined by our professional duties, the idea of being laid off or experiencing volatility may be quite disconcerting. Many people view their jobs as a source of fulfillment and meaning in addition to money. The subject of career uncertainty is particularly pertinent to people in all industries and phases of their careers due to the increased instability in the labor market today, which is fueled by technical and economic advancements.

As employment uncertainty may have a significant psychological impact, emotional resilience is essential for overcoming these obstacles. Stress, anxiety, and even depression are frequently brought on by a fear of redundancy, which can hinder decision-making and lower overall productivity. Resilience, or the capacity to bounce back and adjust in the face of hardship, enables people to maintain composure and concentration even in situations that appear out of their control. It is a talent that improves one's capacity to grasp opportunities in the face of uncertainty in addition to protecting mental health.

In a changing workplace, flexibility is equally important. Individuals' capacity to adapt to external disturbances is determined by their capacity to alter course, pick up new abilities, and welcome change. The problems of a changing labor market are better met by those who have a development mentality, which sees mistakes as teaching moments rather than failures. This viewpoint supports employees in preserving their feeling of autonomy and hope, which is critical for both career growth and individual wellbeing.

Taking proactive measures is also essential for handling professional uncertainty. Career resilience may be improved by developing a strong professional network, seeking further education, and keeping up with market developments. By fostering a sense of control and increasing employability, these measures lessen the helplessness that sometimes accompanies job uncertainty. Employees who take initiative may change their emphasis from things they cannot control to things they can, which gives them a sense of purpose and empowerment.

Perhaps the most crucial—yet difficult—aspect of managing job instability is preserving mental health during uncertain times. Reducing stress and keeping a sense of fulfillment requires mindfulness practices, professional or peer support, and a good work-life balance. By placing a high priority on emotional well-being and self-care, people may withstand changes in their careers without sacrificing their general quality of life.

A wider understanding of the necessity of striking a balance between one's emotional and professional goals is reflected in the increased interest in this subject. Developing the inner fortitude and coping mechanisms required to thrive in the face of adversity is more important for modern workplace success than just surviving outside interruptions. Addressing these concerns is crucial for both individuals and businesses in order to create a workforce that is not just competent and effective but also resilient, content, and prepared to face the future with assurance.

1.3. The Landscape of Job Security

For many years, job security has been a fundamental component of both financial stability and self-assurance, forming the basis of a stable and secure existence. It has always been associated with assurances of stable work, predictable income, and long-term benefits like retirement plans, health insurance, and pensions. Much of the workforce in the 20th century was expected to work for one company for decades, advance through the ranks of that company, and retire with a pension. The social compact between employers and employees, which placed a premium on loyalty and long-term commitment, strong labor markets, and union rights all served to further solidify this feeling of security.

However, due to changes in economic systems, technological breakthroughs, globalization, and evolving workplace dynamics, the idea of job security has experienced significant changes in recent years. Lifetime work is becoming less common as a result of factors including automation, outsourcing, and the growth of the gig economy that have overturned traditional employment structures. At the same time, expectations in society have changed, placing more value on adaptability, creativity, and lifelong learning than on fixed roles and routines.

Today, job security is less about guaranteed employment with a single employer and more about employability—the ability to remain relevant, adaptable, and competitive in an ever-changing job market. This shift places greater emphasis on acquiring transferable skills, staying abreast of industry trends, and embracing lifelong learning to navigate career transitions effectively. For many, the modern workforce demands resilience and agility, as individuals are often required to pivot between roles, industries, and even career paths to maintain their livelihoods and achieve professional growth.

1.4. The Evolving Definition of Job Security

As the workforce undergoes a paradigm shift, job security is becoming more and more dependent on the person rather than the business. While old models depended on employers to offer long-term stability through consistent employment, benefits, and career advancement, modern workers are expected to take charge of their own professional development. This change has made it more important for people to take personal responsibility for their professional growth, as success now depends on their capacity to adjust to changing labor market needs.

Skills, adaptability, and networking have emerged as the new pillars of job security, replacing the traditional guarantees of tenure and organizational loyalty. Continuous learning and skill development are essential for maintaining relevance, as industries are rapidly transformed by technology, automation, and globalization. Adaptability has become critical, enabling workers to pivot effectively in response to market changes, new technologies, and emerging opportunities. Networking, both online and offline, is now a vital strategy for accessing job openings, mentorship, and collaboration, highlighting the importance of relationships in career advancement. For many, job security is no longer a static state but rather a continuous process of growth, self-improvement, and strategic positioning in an increasingly dynamic and competitive landscape. Accordingly, people must develop a proactive approach to career management, building resilience and agility to thrive in an era of uncertainty, rather than depending on external assurances.

1.5. The Decline of Lifelong Employment

The conventional idea of lifetime employment, which was formerly associated with financial stability and individual safety, has significantly diminished due to significant shifts in the global labor market. Globalization, technology improvements, and changing economic priorities have all contributed to this change, which has made room for more flexible and dynamic employment arrangements. Staying competitive in a dynamic market now require businesses to embrace flexible workforce structures, giving flexibility precedence over stability in their personnel plans. The period of constant, long-term work in a particular sector is obsolete.

Outsourcing to nations with cheaper labor costs and the widespread use of technology have had a substantial impact on jobs that formerly offered stability, especially in industries like manufacturing. In many conventional sectors, the need for human labor has decreased due to simplified operations triggered by the industrialization of repetitive work and the development of artificial intelligence. For workers who formerly depended on these industries for long-term careers, this has resulted in a significant decrease in the availability of professions that once held the promise of lifetime employment, causing uncertainty.

Workers have been forced to accept more ephemeral and flexible career choices in reaction to these shifts, abandoning expectations of permanency. Many increasingly explore chances in gig or freelance economies, short-term contract employment, and positions in developing areas that need constant skill development and adaptation. In addition to modifying people's perceptions of job security, this development has reshaped career advancement by focusing more on adaptability, resilience, and the ability to deal with a constantly shifting work environment. Many believe that adopting a mindset of constant learning and actively managing one's profession to adjust to the changing demands of the contemporary economy are necessary for success in this new world.

1.6. The Rise of the Gig Economy

The move away from traditional job stability is best shown by the gig economy. The gig economy, which is defined by temporary, task-based labor, has grown tremendously as a result of online marketplaces that link independent contractors with customers. Gig labor has become more popular thanks to companies like Uber, Fiverr, and Task Rabbit. While it offers flexibility, it also lacks the stability that comes with regular positions. Although gig labor is ideal for people who want flexibility and a variety of revenue sources, it frequently has little perks, unpredictable earnings, and few safeguards, which makes it difficult to consider it as a viable long-term security model.

In a similar vein, contract employment has grown in popularity, presenting both possibilities and difficulties. As contracts enable businesses to control expenses and grow their personnel in response to demand, employers are favoring them over permanent employment. Contracts may expose employees to a variety of projects and sectors, but there are hazards involved. The sense of security that traditional work previously offered can be undermined by stress and financial uncertainty brought on by limited job stability, absence of benefits, and the persistent urge to seize the next opportunity.

A further noteworthy development in the job market is freelancing. Freelancing, made possible by digital technology and global connectivity, allows people to provide specialized talents to clients directly without the involvement of an employer. Employees are empowered by this paradigm to set their own conditions, select their own initiatives, and develop their own personal brands. But it also completely places the onus of job stability on the individual. Without the safety nets offered by regular employment, freelancers frequently have to handle their own benefits, taxes, and retirement planning.

1.7. Benefits and Drawbacks of the New Models

Although traditional employment models sometimes lack the flexibility and autonomy that the gig economy, contract work, and freelancing provide, they also bring with them special difficulties that can make striking a balance between work and personal life more difficult. Many people are drawn to the freedom of scheduling their own time, choosing interesting tasks, and eschewing strict corporate structures. But there are a lot of trade-offs associated with this freedom, especially when it comes to one's psychological well-being and financial security.

A major obstacle is the absence of steady income and conventional benefits like health insurance, paid time off, or retirement plans. Significant stress can result from this financial uncertainty, particularly during recessions or times when employment possibilities are limited. Furthermore, the responsibility for financial planning, tax management, and benefit acquisition rests entirely on the individual, necessitating a degree of financial understanding and proactive management that many people may find intimidating.

These job patterns are further complicated by the obligation to continuously market oneself, attract clients, and uphold a professional reputation. In order to produce high-quality work, freelancers and gig workers frequently have to balance several responsibilities, including those of marketer, accountant, strategist, and service provider. This can make it tough to distinguish between business and personal life because of the digital age's continual connectedness, which makes it hard to "clock out." When the lines between work and leisure time blur, burnout becomes a serious concern.

For many, these models provide opportunities to build a more tailored and fulfilling career path, aligning work with personal values, interests, or life circumstances. However, they demand significant self-discipline, time management, and risk tolerance. Individuals must be willing to embrace uncertainty and adapt to changing market demands, often without the safety nets that traditional employment provides.

These compromises demonstrate how job security is evolving in the contemporary economy. A larger cultural shift is reflected in the drift away from institutional support—such as steady incomes and long-term benefits toward a model that places more emphasis on individual initiative and an entrepreneurial spirit. Resilience, a proactive commitment to professional growth, and the capacity to negotiate the intricacies of a workforce that is becoming more and more independent and self-reliant are necessary for success in this setting.

1.8. Societal Impacts of the Shift

This shift in job security models has a significant impact on society and is changing how governments, businesses, and individuals approach social and economic well-being. Traditional benefits like health insurance, retirement plans, and paid time off – which were once a mainstay of employer-employee contracts, are increasingly being delegated to individual responsibility or linked to government initiatives. A clear gap in access to financial security has resulted from this shift, especially for people in low-income contract or gig jobs that lack the safeguards of regular employment.

Lack of access to benefits like employer-sponsored retirement savings or reasonably priced healthcare sometimes pushes people in unstable professions to rely on inadequate public safety nets, which exacerbates societal inequality. Individuals who are unable to prepare for retirement or get private insurance are more vulnerable during illness, recessions, or later life stages. Marginalized populations are more likely to work in the gig economy or other precarious job sectors, which exacerbates these imbalances and feeds cycles of poverty and financial instability.

The loss of employment security has serious psychological and emotional repercussions in addition to financial ones. Chronic stress and anxiety can result from the uncertainty of one's next paycheck's source as well as the ongoing need to promote oneself, look for new possibilities, and stay competitive. Long-term planning and a sense of personal control are undermined by this unpredictability, which makes it hard for people to feel confident about their futures. These pressures have the potential to exacerbate physical health conditions, lower work satisfaction, and mental health disorders over time.

These changes force communities, organizations, and governments to reconsider support systems and regulations on a societal level. The increasing disparities and volatility in the workforce are being addressed by innovations like universal basic income, transferable benefits, and increased access to public healthcare. The significant ramifications of this shift highlight the necessity of teamwork to prevent disadvantaged groups from being left behind by the changing nature of work while also promoting opportunity and resilience in a changing economic environment.

1.9. Building a New Framework for Job Security

In order to successfully navigate this rapidly evolving job landscape, governments and workers alike must adopt a forward-thinking strategy that places a high value on resilience, equality, and adaptation. Employees must now pursue lifetime learning and ongoing skill improvement in order to be competitive in a labor market that is always changing. People must embrace innovation, be flexible in their jobs, and constantly upskill due to the rapid speed of technology breakthroughs, automation, and changing market expectations. To do this, you must not only learn new technical skills but also cultivate soft skills like communication, problem-solving, and flexibility, which are becoming more and more important in all sectors of the economy.

However, the responsibility for adapting to these changes cannot rest solely on the shoulders of workers. Employers and governments have a critical role to play in fostering a workforce that is prepared for the demands of the modern economy. Employers must take the lead in creating supportive environments by offering training programs, mentorship opportunities, and access to resources that enable employees to grow and thrive. For gig and contract workers, who often operate outside traditional employment structures, companies can implement fair practices by providing protections such as minimum wage standards, paid leave, and pathways to professional development.

Governments also have a key role in making sure that new employment patterns are egalitarian, equitable, and inclusive. The increasing gap between security and flexibility can be bridged by policymakers through the implementation of creative solutions adapted to the needs of the contemporary workforce. The need stability can be achieved by offering benefits that are transferable, including health insurance, retirement savings plans, and unemployment insurance that accompany employees, to those in gig and freelance jobs. Governments may also impose laws that safeguard employees' rights in unconventional work arrangements, making sure that flexibility doesn't compromise equity or financial stability.

A more inclusive and equitable future for all can be achieved through promoting public-private partnerships to address workforce gaps, encourage entrepreneurship, and increase access to technology. Inclusive economic policies are essential for addressing disparities in access to opportunities. Investments in education, reasonably priced childcare, and infrastructure that facilitates remote work can help workers from diverse backgrounds fully participate in the changing economy.

By combining these initiatives, it will be possible to create a dynamic, sustainable, and empowering work environment that bridges the gap between the freedom that workers increasingly enjoy and the much desired security. In this new age of labor, civilizations may guarantee that workers not only survive but flourish by coordinating individual endeavors with group efforts.

1.10 The Future of Job Security

A confluence of economic changes, shifting cultural objectives, and technology improvements is likely to continue to rapidly alter the job security picture. Digital transformation, automation, and artificial intelligence are changing sectors, making some old occupations obsolete but also generating new ones. These factors, together with globalization and changing consumer needs, are causing contemporary workforce to become more flexible, dispersed, and dynamic than it has ever been. As these developmental events unfold, the conventional idea of lifetime work is being replaced by a more adaptable and flexible model that places an emphasis on skills, creativity, and ongoing education rather than security and tenure.

Although this change has caused disruptions in the workforce, it also presents new opportunities for development, ingenuity, and fortitude. Those who are open to change might pursue intriguing job paths in emerging fields including technology, health innovation, and renewable energy. Employees that make the effort to acquire transferable skills, have an open mind to interdisciplinary prospects, and already actively managing the unpredictabilities of the contemporary labor market. Success in this new workplace environment will increasingly be determined by one's capacity to change course, adopt technology, and innovate.

At the same time, the evolving definition of job security challenges society to rethink and reimagine its framework for supporting workers. Employers, policymakers, and educational institutions must collaborate to equip individuals with the tools and resources needed to navigate this changing landscape. This includes providing access to affordable education, fostering environments that encourage lifelong learning, and ensuring equitable access to the digital infrastructure that underpins much of the modern economy. Policies that support entrepreneurship, innovation, and economic inclusion can help create pathways for those traditionally marginalized by rapid workforce changes.

Society may circumvent the constraints of the past and create a more inclusive, adaptable, and sustainable framework for the future by rethinking what security in the modern workplace means to workers. This new strategy can prioritize people's potential first, support a variety of career paths, and give employees a sense of empowerment as they adjust to a workplace that is constantly evolving. Collectively, these paradigm shifts have the potential to create a workforce that is both motivated by the potential of the future and ready for its challenges.

1.10 The Impact of Redundancy:

A strong feeling of loss frequently accompanies redundancy, which is a reality for many in the unstable work market of today. Redundancy has an emotional, social, and economical impact on people in addition to its immediate effects on jobs. The impact on relationships, mental health, and general well-being is profound, despite the fact that it is frequently perceived as a solely economic occurrence. To address the difficulties posed by layoffs and promote resilience among those impacted, it is imperative that individuals, businesses, and legislators have a thorough understanding of these repercussions.

The emotional impact of redundancy can be devastating, often triggering feelings of failure, inadequacy, and rejection. For many, their job is intertwined with their identity, and losing it can lead to a loss of purpose and self-worth. Anxiety about the future, coupled with the stigma sometimes attached to unemployment, can exacerbate feelings of stress and depression. The uncertainty surrounding finances, career prospects, and the ability to meet familial obligations can weigh heavily on individuals, affecting their mental health and decision-making abilities.

1.10.1. Social Consequences

The social fallout from redundancy frequently extends much beyond the person who is immediately impacted. The emotional and economic challenges of unemployment can put further strain on relationships with friends and family. Feelings of insecurity, annoyance, or low self-esteem can cause stress in even the strongest relationships as family members and friends try to support the person through this trying period.

Additionally, the stigma that frequently surrounds losing a job may make these difficulties worse by making people withdraw socially out of humiliation or shame, further isolating them at a time assistance is needed the most.

The financial and psychological effects of redundancy can break down communication and family dynamics. For example, concern over sustaining a specific level of life or fulfilling basic necessities may arise from losing a reliable source of income. These worries may lead to disputes about priorities, budgets, or future goals. Parents may experience guilt about not being able to support their kids as well as they used to, and spouses may struggle with the stress of shouldering more financial or emotional responsibilities. When emotions are running high, it can be challenging to have open and sympathetic conversation, which is crucial in these situations.

Friendships may also be affected, as individuals facing redundancy might feel reluctant to share their struggles or worry about being judged. Social interactions that once brought joy and relaxation can become fraught with discomfort if the individual feels they must explain or justify their situation. In some cases, the financial constraints of unemployment may lead to declining invitations to social outings, further isolating the individual and creating a sense of disconnection.

Additionally, redundancy might have important social repercussions in the workplace. Losing a job can cause disruptions to professional networks and negatively impact the individual's sense of belonging since it frequently involves losing regular interactions with mentors and coworkers. During unemployment, these professional relationships that were formerly a source of support and companionship may seem far away or unreachable. Without taking proactive steps to preserve or reestablish professional relationships, people could find it difficult to explore new opportunities, which would make them feel even more isolated and detached from their industry.

Maintaining social ties and a strong support system during redundancy is crucial but often challenging. Reaching out to family and friends, even when it feels difficult, can provide emotional support and a sense of stability. Sharing feelings and concerns openly with trusted loved ones can alleviate some of the burden and foster understanding. Support groups or community organizations tailored to individuals facing unemployment can also offer camaraderie, practical advice, and a space to connect with others navigating similar challenges.

Using internet resources such as LinkedIn can aid in reestablishing and fortifying professional networks. Proactive strategies to remain involved and visible include joining professional associations, going to industry events, and keeping in touch with former coworkers. In addition to offering insightful information about new prospects, informational interviews and mentorship programs may aid in restoring confidence.

While redundancy is unarguably a difficult and lonely experience, it nevertheless presents a chance to reassess and reestablish social ties. People may combat the social effects of losing their jobs and build a better basis for both professional and personal development by actively preserving professional relationships, encouraging open communication, and looking for supporting networks. In addition to lessening the immediate effects of redundancy, these initiatives create the framework for long-term success and resilience.

1.10.2. Financial Instability

Perhaps the most obvious and immediate effect of redundancy is financial difficulty, which has an impact on almost every element of a person's life. For people who have little savings, debt, or financial obligations like dependents, a sudden loss of income can be extremely stressful. People may struggle to pay for necessities like groceries, utilities, rent or a mortgage, transportation, and medical expenditures if they don't have a reliable source of income. People who are under financial duress frequently have to make tough choices, such reducing the size of their living space, cutting down on essentials, or using credit to make ends meet, which can result in debt that keeps getting worse.

Many people find that redundancy also interferes with long-term financial planning, which has repercussions that go beyond the current crisis. For example, when people use their retirement savings to pay for everyday needs, they may exhaust them too soon, endangering their future financial stability. Similar to this, failing to make mortgage, credit card, or loan payments can result in declining credit ratings, which can make it harder to get future financial aid or advantageous conditions. Financial troubles are made worse by the loss of employer-sponsored benefits like health insurance, as people may have to pay for coverage on their own or skip it completely, leaving them more vulnerable to unanticipated medical costs.

The longer the unemployed duration, the more severe the financial effect of redundancy. Long-term job searches can deplete a person's money, leaving them less equipped to handle unforeseen obstacles or fresh chances. Even after obtaining new work, people may find it more difficult to regain their financial stability due to the stress of extended unemployment, which can also result in feelings of economic instability and low confidence.

Beyond the personal consequences, redundancy can have broader societal implications, including increased reliance on social safety nets such as unemployment benefits, food assistance, or subsidized housing. These systems, while critical in providing short-term relief, may not fully address the long-term challenges faced by individuals struggling to recover financially. Addressing the financial fallout of redundancy requires a multifaceted approach, including stronger safety nets, access to affordable retraining programs, and financial education to help individuals build resilience and prepare for potential disruptions in the future.

1.10.3. The Broader Impact on Families

Redundancy has a significant impact on families as well as individuals, frequently changing the social, emotional, and financial aspects of the home. The well-being of parents' children can be greatly impacted by an unexpected loss of income. As families find it difficult to pay for tuition, school materials, or even secure housing in strong school districts, educational plans may be interrupted. Opportunities for social engagement, skill development, and personal growth may be limited if access to extracurricular activities like sports, music classes, or tutoring is restricted. Children may not completely comprehend the situation, but they may nevertheless experience the impacts of the household's financial burden, which might cause them to feel frustrated or lost.

Redundancy's emotional toll on the affected person frequently affects family interactions, causing tension and stress in the home. Relationship-stressing behaviors like impatience, irritability, withdrawal, or emotional detachment might be signs of an individual's feelings of dissatisfaction, inadequacy, or worry. When dealing with their own anxieties and concerns about the future, partners may find it difficult to assist one another, which might result in miscommunication, conflict, or misunderstandings. If the redundancy results in major lifestyle adjustments, such downsizing possessions, relocating to a less costly house, or reducing family activities like celebrations or vacations, these tensions may worsen.

Extended family members and dependents may also experience the anxiety and uncertainty that come with redundancy. Children may become anxious, suffer academically, or exhibit behavioral changes as a result of observing their parents' anxiety. Partners who were not the major breadwinners, on the other hand, can have more pressure to make financial contributions and frequently take on additional work or obligations in order to make ends meet. Losing income can make it more difficult for families with elderly or disabled relatives to get the care, drugs, or other services they need, which can further strain the family.

Redundancy can ultimately make a household's overall stability more unstable, impacting not just the family's short-term financial security but also its long-term cohesiveness and health. To overcome these obstacles, one must be able to communicate openly, solve problems together, ask for help, and accept external assistance, whether it comes from professional counseling services, community resources, or extended family. The effects of redundancy can be lessened and a foundation for healing and development can be established by taking proactive steps like creating an emergency fund or encouraging resilience in family interactions.

1.11. Recovery and Resilience

Even though redundancy can be difficult, it can also be a great opportunity for personal development and reinvention, giving people the chance to reevaluate their goals and set new course. Redundancy offers many people an opportunity to reassess their career objectives, take into account hobbies they had not previously considered, and identify areas in which they need to grow professionally. It may inspire people to learn new skills, seek more education, or change careers completely, giving them a new feeling of direction and purpose. Unexpected possibilities, such freelancing, entrepreneurship, or positions that better fit one's talents, beliefs and ambitions, may arise during this time of introspection.

During this time of transition, emotional resilience is essential as it helps people adjust to change, keep hopes alive, show optimism, and deal with the uncertainty of losing their job. Developing resilience frequently entails concentrating on one's own strengths, establishing realistic objectives, and being positively minded despite failures. People can be empowered to embrace future opportunities and take proactive measures toward rebuilding their careers by cultivating a growth mindset, which sees redundancy as a chance for progress rather than a failure.

Managing the practical and emotional difficulties of redundancy can be greatly improved by seeking expert assistance. Services for career counseling can offer helpful advice on determining transferable skills, honing job search strategies, and interview preparation. These services frequently assist people in grasping market trends and investigating potential job options that they may not have previously thought of. Equally crucial is mental health care, such as therapy or counseling, which provides a secure environment for processing feelings like sadness, anger, or worry while developing coping mechanisms to control stress and stay focused.

Navigating this changeover phase can also be greatly aided by networking and community assistance. Making connections with peers, mentors, or professional associations may make people feel less isolated, motivate them, and open doors to new opportunities. Many discover that, despite its first disruptive effects, redundancy eventually promotes personal development, increased self-awareness, and the acquisition of abilities and connections that improve both their personal and professional life. People might transform a difficult experience into a springboard for a more satisfying future by accepting this time as a chance for reinvention.

1.12. Role of Employers and Society

Employers may help lessen the effects of redundancy by providing for the immediate needs of impacted workers as well as by encouraging a culture of accountability and empathy in trying times. A crucial first step is transparent communication, which guarantees that staff members are aware of upcoming changes as soon as possible. Even in challenging situations, providing straightforward, sincere justifications for redundancy may foster confidence and lessen uncertainly. Giving workers prior notice gives them a good start in preparing their future steps by allowing them to emotionally, financially, and professionally prepare.

Another essential tool that organizations may use to facilitate the transition is outplacement services. These services, which enable workers to reenter the labor market with confidence and support, frequently include career counseling, resume development, job search aid, and interview preparation. Giving people access to mental health tools, including stress management courses or counseling, can help them deal with the psychological effects of losing their job and build resilience during a time of major transition. The feeling of overwhelm that sometimes accompanies redundancy can be lessened by providing employees with financial planning seminars or consultations that can help them manage their money, deal with current issues, and make future plans.

In order to help people during times of change, society as a whole must work to establish strong safety nets. While people look for new possibilities, unemployment benefits help them meet their basic necessities by acting as a vital financial cushion. In a labor market that is evolving rapidly, retraining programs and workforce development efforts are equally crucial since they provide avenues for skill improvement and career pivoting. To ensure that workers are ready for future possibilities, these programs should be easily available, reasonably priced, and customized to meet the needs of the labor market and growing sectors.

Another essential component of successful assistance is affordable healthcare, which guarantees that people and families may continue to have access to essential medical services even in the event that employer-sponsored coverage are eliminated. Redundancy may be especially disastrous in nations where healthcare is linked to employment, highlighting the need for policies that separate health coverage from employment status. Peer support groups, networking gatherings, and local job fairs are examples of community-based programs that may be very helpful in providing people with opportunities, resources, and support throughout their transition.

Employers and society at large may lessen the negative effects of redundancy by giving priority to these strategies, turning a potentially upsetting event into a chance for development, resiliency, and reinvention. When combined, these initiatives produce a more encouraging framework that respects the reality of contemporary work while enabling people to face uncertain times with dignity and confidence.

1.13 Moving Forward

Despite being extremely disruptive, redundancy is not an insurmountable obstacle. It is a major life event that may affect people on many levels, but recovery and resilience are possible with the correct help and techniques. The first step in developing significant solutions that empower impacted people and fortify communities is acknowledging the complex emotional, social, and financial aspects of its impact.

Redundancy can cause emotional reactions such as fear, grief, and future uncertainty. In order to assist people process these feelings and regain their confidence, it is essential to promote mental health through easily available counseling, peer support groups, and stress management tools. Strong networks of family, friends, and colleagues in the workplace may offer support, guidance, and useful help during this time of change, so social ties are also quite important. Initiatives initiated by the community, such mentoring programs and networking gatherings, may strengthen these links even further, lowering isolation and creating new opportunities.

Another crucial component of overcoming redundancy is financial recovery. Giving people access to useful services like budgeting tools, financial literacy classes, and emergency grants or unemployment insurance can help them take back control of their financial circumstances. To make sure that safety nets and retraining programs are strong, available, and in line with the changing needs of the job market, governments, companies, and nonprofit groups must collaborate. Initiatives for retraining and upskilling are especially crucial because they allow people to learn new skills and adjust to new sectors, transforming layoffs into chances for professional reinvention.

To turn a time of turmoil into one of opportunity, one must prioritize personal development and flexibility. Professional development courses, certifications, and skill-building programs can enable people to reenter the workforce more competitively and with more strength. Furthermore, encouraging a resilient and positive mentality enables people to see redundancy as an opportunity to pursue novel endeavors, hone their objectives, and find greater fulfillment rather than as a permanent setback. The difficulties of redundancy must ultimately be addressed with teamwork, compassion, and creative thinking. A more flexible and secure workforce of the future—one that values both flexibility and stability—must be developed via cooperation between employers, legislators, and communities. By pooling resources, fostering financial and emotional healing, and placing a strong emphasis on social interaction and skill development, society can turn the experience of redundancy into a springboard for resilience, creativity, and progress.

Chapter 2: Common Fears Around Job Security

2.1. Common Fears Around Job Security

Many people experience deep-seated, fundamental worries that go well beyond the immediate difficulties of financial instability when they consider the risk of losing their jobs. The psychological and social aspects of work insecurity are just as important but less frequently talked about, even while practical concerns like the inability to support one's family or pay for necessities are frequently at the forefront.

Perhaps the most urgent and immediate anxiety is the fear of losing one's income as it has a direct impact on one's capacity to maintain one's level of living, pay bills like rent or a mortgage, and make future plans. However, losing a job can also cause stress by interfering with longer-term financial objectives like developing wealth, supporting school, or preparing for retirement. The possibility of redundancy can be devastating for people who are living paycheck to paycheck or who have substantial financial obligations; it can cause a difficult-to-manage sense of urgency and anxiety.

Job instability touches on deeper psychological worries in addition to these pragmatic ones. Personal identity, self-worth, and a feeling of purpose are frequently entwined with work. Losing a job can cause people to struggle to reframe their value outside of their professional function, and consequently result in feelings of inadequacy, guilt, or a lack of direction. Those who have devoted years to a single organization or profession may experience this loss of identity more acutely because their sense of self may be strongly linked to their work. As losing a job can carry a stigma that makes people feel alienated or condemned, social worries also play a role. Employment is strongly associated with success, respectability, and prestige in many communities, and losing one's work can cause emotions of humiliation or failure. People may find it more difficult to ask for assistance or talk to others about their experiences as a result of these social expectations, which can worsen the emotional toll of redundancy.

Understanding these fears is essential for both individuals and organizations to address the complex realities of job insecurity. For individuals, recognizing and validating these emotions can be the first step toward building resilience and taking proactive steps to prepare for change. Organizations, on the other hand, have a responsibility to support their employees through periods of uncertainty by fostering transparent communication, providing resources for career development, and creating a culture that values adaptability and lifelong learning. By addressing both the tangible and intangible fears associated with job insecurity, society can create a more empathetic and supportive framework that helps individuals navigate the challenges of the modern workforce.

2.1.1. Fear of Losing Income

Among the most obvious and palpable concerns related to job insecurity is the dread of losing one's income, which frequently consumes the minds of individuals who may lose their jobs. An abrupt stop in income can cause people to struggle to pay for essentials like food, utilities, and rent, which can lead to a cascade of financial difficulties. For people who are living paycheck to paycheck, when even a little lapse in income can lead to growing expenses, missed payments, and debt buildup, this dread is particularly intense.

These vulnerabilities were brought to light by the COVID-19 epidemic, when millions of workers were unable to fulfill their financial responsibilities due to massive layoffs, which pushed many to rely on food banks, credit cards, and loans to make ends meet. Without a financial safety net, a short-term catastrophe could become a long-term struggle, increasing stress and future-related concern.

Fear of losing money is significantly more serious for families since it affects dependents and their welfare. Parents can be up at night thinking about how they will continue to support their kids' education, health care, and general well-being. The strain is increased when people worry about paying for extracurricular activities, school supplies, or medical care—especially for those who are already dealing with unstable finances. Additionally, financial instability throws off long-term planning, causing families to postpone important objectives like retirement savings, home ownership, or creating a college fund for their kids. The dread is only heightened by the uncertainty around the time it will take to locate a new work and if the new employment will offer equivalent income and benefits.

This widespread fear emphasizes how crucial systemic support and financial readiness are. Even if it's ideal, many people who are currently struggling find it impossible to save for emergencies, forcing them to rely on social assistance or unemployment benefits. Despite their importance, these resources frequently fall short of filling the gap between employment, underscoring the need for more comprehensive social policies to combat income instability. The emotional toll of living with financial insecurity is not much lessened by increased access to unemployment benefits, financial literacy training, and savings-promoting initiatives.

Loss of money can have a significant psychological impact, including despondency, dread of the future, and feelings of inadequacy. The strain of managing unstable finances while looking for a new job has a negative impact on many people's mental health, increasing their risk of anxiety, sadness, and even physical health issues. A multimodal strategy is needed to address these issues, combining systemic policies intended to provide a safety net for people and families with individual financial planning. In order to prevent a short-term setback from turning into a long-term disaster, society may better help people during times of economic instability by acknowledging and addressing the profound worries associated with income loss.

2.1.2. Loss of Identity

Jobs are much more than simply a way to make a living; for many people, they are closely linked to their sense of self and identity. In addition to offering a concrete indicator of success and a sense of belonging, a person's career frequently provides structure, pride, and a sense of purpose. Therefore, losing a job can cause people to have a severe identity crisis as they consider their worth and position in society. This is especially true for those who work in highly specialized, demanding, or prominent positions, where their professional achievements define their sense of self.

An executive who has spent decades working their way up the corporate ladder, for example, may experience a feeling of loss that extends beyond money if they lose their job. For these individuals, their position, duties, or job title are frequently important identifiers; losing these might make them feel disoriented and unconnected. Similar to this, it might be particularly difficult for workers in creative industries like authors, musicians, or painters to separate their own worth from how their work is received. In these situations, losing job or having their career stagnate might feel like a rejection of their abilities and personal value.

The fear of losing one's professional identity can trigger deep emotional responses. Feelings of inadequacy and self-doubt often emerge, as individuals struggle to reconcile their worth with the loss of a role that previously defined them. This can lead to depression, anxiety, and a diminished sense of self-worth, compounding the emotional and psychological toll of unemployment. For some, the loss of identity may also disrupt their social connections and support systems, as workplace interactions and professional networks often form a significant part of their daily lives.

In order to overcome these obstacles, it is essential to have a feeling of purpose that extends beyond employment. Other kinds of identity and fulfillment might come from taking up interests unrelated to one's work, volunteering, building social ties, or taking up hobbies. People may manage the emotional effects of losing their jobs by developing resilience and adopting a more comprehensive sense of self-worth that is not only based on professional accomplishments. In order to help people regain their confidence, look for new possibilities, and rediscover their sense of purpose, support systems like career coaching, peer networks, and counseling may be quite helpful.

Long-term wellbeing ultimately depends on cultivating a balance between one's personal and professional identities. People may better withstand the difficulties of professional changes and preserve a feeling of worth and purpose, especially during uncertain times, by realizing that employment is only one aspect of a multifaceted personality. This viewpoint encourages a more sustainable and satisfying way of living and working in addition to assisting people in adjusting to losing their jobs.

2.1.3. *Fear of the Unknown*

The uncertainty that comes with losing a job frequently feeds a deep and widespread fear of what lies ahead as people struggle with a number of troubling concerns. Some people feel stuck and unwilling to take proactive measures because of paralyzing worries like "How long will it take to find a new job?" or "Will I have to switch industries?" Those who have worked in sectors like manufacturing, retail, or the media that are experiencing major change are particularly affected by this dread of the unknown. Anxiety has increased as a result of the rapid speed at which automation, technical breakthroughs, and global economic changes have left many people doubting their capacity to adjust to new positions or sectors.

For example, the idea of retraining or acquiring completely new skills may be daunting to a manufacturing worker who has worked for decades in a position that is now being automated. Lack of exposure to the technology or procedures influencing the modern workplace frequently exacerbates this concern, making the transition to a new professional path appear unachievable. In a similar vein, older workers may be concerned that their current skill set is out of date and makes them inadequately suited for the needs of the modern workforce. The very real worry about age-related bias adds to this stress since older workers frequently experience (and occasionally witness) discrimination throughout the employment process, which further erodes their self-esteem.

The fear of the unknown encompasses not only age or skill levels but also negotiating unfamiliar ground in a work market that is extremely competitive and changing quickly. This fear frequently results from a lack of trust in one's capacity to adjust and thrive in novel situations. People can question their ability to pick up new skills, acquire new technology, or compete with younger, tech-savvy applicants. Because the uncertainty appears too great to face head-on, the overwhelming nature of these difficulties might cause emotions of powerlessness, procrastination, or avoidance.

Nevertheless this anxiety also highlights how crucial flexibility and lifelong learning are becoming in today's workforce. Workers in all industries are finding that the capacity to adapt to change, pick up new skills, and seize new opportunities is an essential survival skill. Many people need access to helpful tools, such reasonably priced retraining programs, mentoring opportunities, and professional counseling, in order to overcome their fear of the unknown. For those facing job changes, community institutions, online learning environments, and government programs that offer affordable, flexible education and skill-building courses can be a lifeline.

Addressing these anxieties requires developing resilience and self-assurance. Soft skill development programs that emphasize problem-solving, critical thinking, and flexibility might enable employees to face change with hope rather than fear. Professional networks and peer support groups may offer motivation and helpful guidance, assisting people in viewing their difficulties as chances for personal development rather than insurmountable roadblocks.

In the end, even though fear of the unknown is a normal reaction to losing a job, it may be lessened with planning, knowledge, and mental adjustment. Individuals and society as a whole may turn uncertainty into a springboard for innovation and advancement by encouraging flexibility and a dedication to lifelong learning. This strategy not only reduces workers' immediate fear of losing their jobs, but it also gives them the skills they need to succeed in a changing and uncertain labor market.

2.2. Comparisons and Social Stigma

In a world where professional achievement is frequently connected with personal value, losing a job frequently entails the fear of being evaluated or negatively compared to others. Unemployment might feel like a very personal failure in such a setting, making people susceptible to emotions of guilt and inadequacy. These feelings are exacerbated by the stigma associated with losing a job, which makes people feel alone because they fear that their peers, family, or even prospective employers would view them as incompetent or unworthy.

This fear is particularly pronounced in a world increasingly dominated by social media, where people frequently flaunt their achievements and milestones for public consumption. For example, a young professional who loses their job might find it difficult to scroll through platforms filled with announcements of promotions, career achievements, or professional accolades from friends and acquaintances. The curated and celebratory nature of social media can amplify feelings of inadequacy, as it often paints an unrealistic picture of success while omitting struggles or setbacks. This comparison can lead to heightened self-doubt and a reluctance to share one's own challenges, reinforcing the sense of isolation.

The tremendous pressure to uphold a façade of achievement might deter people from asking for help or being candid about their difficulties. Many decide to suffer in silence out of fear of being judged or rejected rather than asking for assistance or guidance. In addition to making the emotional toll of losing a job worse, this silence keeps people from getting access to important tools that may help them recover, such networking opportunities, career counseling, and mental health assistance.

The constant fear of being judged emphasizes how urgently a culture change that normalizes job losses and promotes empathy and understanding is needed. Losing a job is a normal aspect of the current work environment, which is becoming more unpredictable and dynamic. It should not be seen as a sign of personal failure. Public awareness campaigns, workplace projects, and educational activities can all help dispel the stigma attached to unemployment. By showcasing examples of resiliency and reinvention, for instance, we may influence people to see job loss as a chance for personal development rather than a cause for embarrassment.

The irrational expectations that fuel social stigma can also be dismantled by encouraging candid discussions about the realities of the labor market. People can obtain support and encouragement from others who have gone through similar struggles by sharing their stories in safe places offered via online and offline support networks. By assisting former employees with outplacement services and positive recommendations and by treating job changes as normal, employers may also play a role.

In the end, overcoming the fear of social stigma and comparisons calls for collective effort. Society may assist people in overcoming the emotional difficulties of losing a job with dignity and confidence by normalizing professional losses and fostering empathetic and supportive cultures. This can transform what may at first seem like a failure into an opportunity for personal development and growth.

2.3. Strategic Coping Mechanisms and Resilience

A diversified strategy is needed to address these anxieties. Developing emotional resilience on a personal level is essential. Self-reflection, therapy, and mindfulness are among techniques that might help people deal with the stress and anxiety caused by the uncertainties associated with unemployment. For instance, people might regain their confidence and consider other options if they redefine losing their work as a chance for personal development rather than a failure.

Proactively developing skills and networking are also essential. Online platforms, professional associations, and mentorship programs provide opportunities to learn, connect, and discover new career paths. For instance, an individual transitioning from a declining industry to a growing field like technology can benefit from online courses or certification programs, which can build the confidence needed to navigate the unknown.

Addressing fears of job insecurity requires robust policy and societal interventions that go beyond individual solutions to create comprehensive safety nets and foster a supportive environment for workers navigating economic transitions. Strengthening unemployment benefits is a critical first step, ensuring that individuals who lose their jobs have access to financial support that covers basic living expenses while they search for new opportunities. Expanding access to affordable healthcare is equally important, as losing a job often means losing employer-sponsored benefits. Decoupling healthcare from employment can significantly reduce the financial and emotional strain on individuals and families, providing a more stable foundation during periods of job loss.

Initiatives for workforce development and subsidized retraining are crucial for assisting employees in adjusting to the quickly shifting needs of the contemporary labor market. These programs can give people the skills they need to transition into new careers by providing accessible, reasonably priced training in cutting-edge industries including technology, renewable energy, and healthcare. "Flexicurity" policies, which combine robust social safeguards like state-funded retraining programs and large jobless compensation with flexible labor markets, have been effectively adopted by nations like Denmark. Because of this concept, employees may move between roles more confidently, which lowers their fear of losing their jobs and promotes an adaptable culture.

Equally crucial are public initiatives that promote the idea of career reinvention and reduce the shame associated with losing one's job. As earlier mentioned, losing a job is frequently seen by society as a personal failure rather than a normal aspect of a changing economy, which might deter people from asking for assistance or looking into other options. This narrative may be changed by campaigns that tell tales of resiliency and achievement following job loss, inspiring individuals to see redundancy as a chance for personal development rather than a permanent setback. These initiatives may be strengthened by establishing forums for candid discussions about job instability, normalizing conversations about the psychological and practical difficulties of unemployment, and encouraging a feeling of community.

Another important strategy is to promote cooperation between employers, governments, and educational institutions. Partnerships between the public and commercial sectors can finance retraining initiatives, offer mentorship programs, and open doors to jobs in industries with high demand. Incentives for businesses that hire personnel from displaced industries or engage in employee development can also help allay fears about job security while fostering economic expansion.

Building resilience at the individual and systemic levels must be the ultimate goal of societal and policy initiatives. These interventions may help employees move between jobs with confidence and build a more flexible, safe workforce by bolstering safety nets, lowering stigma, and encouraging lifelong learning. In addition to helping people, this all-encompassing strategy promotes a more just and sustainable economy.

2.4. Conclusion

The fears surrounding job security—loss of income, identity, fear of the unknown, and social stigma—are deeply intertwined with human emotions and societal norms. While these fears are natural, they can be mitigated through a combination of individual resilience, organizational support, and systemic change. By fostering adaptability, empathy, and innovation, individuals and society can redefine the concept of job security for the modern era, transforming challenges into opportunities for growth and fulfillment.

Chapter 3: The Psychological and Emotional Toll

3.1. The Psychological and Emotional Toll

Workers are sometimes left in a state of continual uncertainty due to the widespread anxiety surrounding job insecurity. This is frequently exacerbated by the ongoing possibility of layoffs, organizational reorganization, or changes in market circumstances. Chronic stress can result from the need to demonstrate one's indispensable status in such a setting, as people feel pressured to put in more hours, take on more duties, or perform better than expected in order to maintain their jobs. In addition to undermining work-life balance, this "always-on" mindset has a negative impact on mental health.

Stress is one of the most immediate and common outcomes of job insecurity. The fear of losing a job can trigger a fight-or-flight response, leading to physiological symptoms such as insomnia, headaches, or digestive issues. Over time, this heightened state of stress can contribute to more severe health problems, including hypertension, heart disease, and a weakened immune system. Anxiety often accompanies this stress, with individuals worrying not only about their current roles but also about their ability to secure future employment if the worst should happen. The unpredictable nature of job insecurity exacerbates these feelings, creating a sense of helplessness and lack of control.

Another frequent result of ongoing employment uncertainty is depression. A person's sense of purpose and self-worth may be undermined by the worry of being laid off, especially if their identity is strongly linked to their work. Demotivation and productivity can be further reduced by the emergence of feelings of inadequacy, worthlessness, and pessimism. Some people have such an unbearable emotional toll that they retreat from social and professional circles, cutting them off from possible support networks.

Avoidance behaviors often emerge as a coping mechanism for dealing with the uncertainty of job insecurity. Rather than confronting their fears, some individuals may disengage from their work, avoid difficult conversations with supervisors, or shy away from opportunities to build their skills or networks. While these behaviors may provide temporary relief, they can also exacerbate the problem by reducing performance and visibility, potentially making them more vulnerable to job loss.

The widespread occurrence of these emotional difficulties emphasizes how urgently management and impact-reduction techniques are needed. Stress-reduction methods including mindfulness, physical activity, and counseling can help people become more resilient and keep their emotional equilibrium. It is also the duty of organizations to provide supportive workplaces by encouraging open communication, offering tools for mental health, and minimizing needless job instability through open decision-making and equitable hiring procedures.

Both people and organizations may contribute to the creation of healthier, more productive workplaces by addressing these psychological and emotional components of job insecurity. This will enable employees to manage difficult times with more self-assurance and wellbeing.

3.1.1. Stress and Burnout

Stress is one of the most widespread psychological impacts of job instability, especially in settings where workers feel pressured to put in extra hours in order to avoid being seen as disposable. When people overcommit out of anxiety to prove their worth to the company, they may push themselves over their breaking point, which can result in burnout. In order to maintain their job amid downsizing, an employee at a computer business going through restructuring, for instance, would put in extra hours and take on more duties.

The same efforts people undertake to safeguard their careers may trigger burnout, which is characterized by emotional tiredness, alienation, and decreased productivity. Employees become less motivated, more prone to make errors, and more likely to have interpersonal disputes when their mental and physical health deteriorates. Ironically, these consequences can lead to a vicious cycle in which burnout lowers performance and may increase a person's susceptibility to layoffs. In order to address burnout, firms must change their culture to value work-life balance and assist staff in efficiently handling their duties.

3.1.2. Anxiety and Depression

A pervasive sense of uncertainty, which can take the form of anxiety and melancholy, is fostered by the ongoing prospect of layoffs. Questions about when or if layoffs will happen, if one will be impacted, and how to handle life after losing a job are some of the unknowns that frequently cause anxiety. This hypervigilance can exacerbate stress by causing physical symptoms including headaches, sleeplessness, and digestive problems.

Feelings of worthlessness and powerlessness, on the other side, can lead to depression. The dread of redundancy can cause a deep sense of failure for those whose professional positions are firmly linked to their sense of self. A mid-career professional who worries about being supplanted by younger, tech-savvy employee, for instance, could internalize these worries because they think they are useless in the contemporary workplace. Such ideas have the potential to cause social withdrawal, a decline in interest in hobbies, and a lowered quality of living over time.

3.1.3. Avoidance and Paralysis

Fear of job loss can also result in avoidance behaviors and decision-making paralysis. Many individuals, overwhelmed by the prospect of change, prefer to stay in unsatisfactory roles rather than proactively explore new opportunities. This avoidance stems from a fear of failure, where the risks associated with change appear greater than the discomfort of staying in a precarious situation.

An employee in a deteriorating industry, for example, can be reluctant to change to a more stable business or seek new training because they are afraid of starting again. This hesitancy might hinder professional advancement and make it more difficult for the person to adjust to changing market needs. Avoidance behaviors can also show up in daily chores, when workers are reluctant to take charge or make choices out of concern that they could make mistakes that could cost them their jobs.

The culture of the workplace has a significant impact on how workers perceive and manage job insecurity. The psychological toll is frequently increased by a poisonous working culture, which fosters an atmosphere of fear and uncertainty. Employees may feel alone, underappreciated, and worried about their prospects in such environments if organizational changes are not communicated openly and competition is prioritized over teamwork. Organizations that do not publicly discuss possible changes during times of restructuring, for example, frequently leave workers wondering and worrying about the worst, which raises stress levels and distrust.

Employee morale and productivity may suffer as a result of this uncertainty as workers may devote more emotional energy to thinking about their job security than to their duties. Toxic cultures may not only increase anxiety but also deter workers from raising issues or asking for help. When companies disregard concerns about job stability or place a higher priority on performance metrics than employee well-being, employees may be reluctant to voice their concerns for fear of judgment or reprisal. People find it more difficult to handle the emotional difficulties of job uncertainty as a result of this silence, which intensifies feelings of loneliness and inadequacy. Additionally, a highly competitive culture that pits people against one another for promotion or recognition can erode team cohesiveness by making workers feel disposable and unsupported.

On the other hand, the detrimental impacts of job instability may be considerably lessened by a supportive workplace culture. An environment of mutual respect and trust is fostered by organizations that place a high value on transparency, regular communication, and appreciation for workers. Giving prompt updates on organizational changes or restructuring plans, for instance, might cut down on conjecture and needless worry. Even in difficult times, open lines of communication that allow staff members to freely voice their worries or ask questions provide a sense of empowerment and inclusion.

A strong workplace culture also includes chances for feedback and recognition of staff members. Employee resilience and morale are increased when their sense of worth and belonging is reinforced via individual and team efforts. Organizations may measure employee sentiment and proactively address problems by using feedback methods like anonymous surveys or frequent check-ins, which demonstrate a sincere commitment to the welfare of their staff.

Furthermore, cultivating a feeling of belonging and a common goal at work might act as a protective barrier against the strain of job uncertainty. Employees who work in collaborative settings prioritizing cooperation, support, and group accomplishment feel more connected and supported, which lessens feelings of loneliness. Companies that provide professional development options, including training courses or career counseling, show their dedication to their employees' development and flexibility by giving them more confidence in their capacity to handle future changes

Finally, it is impossible to overestimate how company culture shapes workers' experiences with job instability. Employees are empowered to tackle uncertainty with resilience and confidence when their organizations foster communication, trust, and a sense of purpose. Employers who prioritize a supportive culture not only boost employee morale and productivity but also create a workforce that is more capable of overcoming the obstacles of a constantly evolving labor market.

The psychological effects of job uncertainty must be managed with proactive, multidimensional coping strategies that take into account both practical and emotional issues. Particularly useful stress-reduction strategies for assisting people in controlling their emotions, preserving mental clarity, and developing resilience include mindfulness, meditation, and physical activity. Engaging in mindfulness exercises helps people to be more present and stop overanalyzing, while regular exercise generates endorphins, which lower stress and elevate mood. These techniques support long-term emotional stability and mental health in addition to helping with short-term stress management.

Addressing emotions of loneliness, helplessness and insecurity requires seeking assistance from peers, mentors, or mental health specialists. Talking with reliable people can help people feel less alone in their troubles by offering perspective, reassurance, and useful counsel. Professional networks or peer support groups can also be helpful for exchanging stories and developing coping mechanisms for job uncertainty. Therapists and counselors are examples of mental health specialists that may provide individualized advice for stress and anxiety management, giving people the skills they need to deal with difficult emotions more skillfully.

Developing a growth mindset is another powerful strategy for navigating uncertainty. A growth mindset involves viewing challenges and setbacks as opportunities for learning and personal development rather than as insurmountable obstacles. By shifting their focus from fear to action, individuals can reclaim a sense of control and empowerment. For example, someone worried about being replaced by automation might choose to proactively upskill by enrolling in technical training courses or certifications that align with emerging industry demands. This not only enhances their employability but also boosts their confidence and adaptability in a rapidly changing job market.

Along with upskilling, people can rediscover their feeling of direction and purpose by establishing small, attainable goals. The process of job reinvention might feel less daunting if more complex issues are broken down into smaller, more doable actions, including updating a résumé, networking with experts, or attending seminars. Maintaining motivation and fending off feelings of stagnation require a sense of success, which is reinforced by celebrating little accomplishments.

Another crucial component of managing job instability is developing financial resilience. People might feel more equipped to handle any unexpected expenses by making a budget, eliminating wasteful spending, and looking for other sources of income like side employment or freelancing. Financial preparation eases the immediate stress brought on by economic uncertainty and offers a sense of security.

Lastly, it's critical to keep a balanced viewpoint. Although worrying about the future is normal, feeling helpless can be lessened by concentrating on things that are under one's control. Journaling, taking up hobbies, or practicing appreciation might help people feel normal and remind them that their worth goes beyond their work identity.

Combining these coping mechanisms helps people better handle the psychological and practical effects of job uncertainty, building resilience and setting themselves up for success in the future. Proactive action reduces the psychological toll and turns uncertainty into a springboard for development and innovation.

3.2. The Role of Leadership in Reducing Stress

Since leaders' communication and team-building techniques have a big impact on employee resilience and morale, leadership is essential to tackling the psychological effects of job instability. In uncertain times, open communication is essential to ensuring that staff members are aware of organizational changes, their possible effects, and the rationale behind them. Open and truthful leaders contribute to the dispelling of rumors and the reduction of speculations, fostering stability even in the face of difficult situations. Since knowledgeable employees are more likely to feel appreciated and respected, this transparency promotes trust.

Effective leadership also requires empathy. Leaders show that they care about the emotional and psychological well of their team by taking the time to listen to and validate their concerns. A supportive work atmosphere may be greatly enhanced by little actions like listening intently, thoughtfully answering questions, and demonstrating empathy for the stress that colleagues may be going through. Stronger bonds are formed between teams and empathetic leaders, who promote candid dialogue and teamwork—two qualities that are essential in unpredictable times.

Another essential component of stress reduction is putting employee well-being first. Leaders who provide their teams access to mental health resources, such wellness seminars, employee support programs, or counseling services, give them the skills they need to deal with the emotional difficulties brought on by job instability. Promoting work-life balance by offering employees remote work choices, flexible scheduling, or scheduled breaks may also reduce stress and support their physical and emotional well-being. In addition to lowering stress, a well-being-promoting workplace culture boosts morale and productivity.

Employees' sense of safety and belonging is further enhanced when they participate in decision-making processes. A manager at a business that is experiencing budget constraints, for instance, may be transparent with their team about the financial difficulties, give frequent updates on the state of affairs, and actively engage staff in finding ways to reduce costs or boost productivity. With this approach, they develop a sense of being active contributors to solutions rather than just passively receiving decisions. Employees who use this collaborative method experience less helplessness and a greater sense of responsibility. Additionally, cooperation fosters trust and reaffirms that management respect staff opinions and knowledge.

Leaders may also combat the negative impacts of job instability by expressing gratitude and acknowledgment. Even in uncertain times, employees feel appreciated and confident in their responsibilities when accomplishments are celebrated, hard work is acknowledged, and constructive criticism is given. Employee morale is raised and their value to the company is emphasized through a recognition culture.

In the end, leadership that prioritizes openness, compassion, and proactive assistance may greatly reduce the stress brought on by job instability. Leaders enable their teams to face uncertainty with resilience and confidence by cultivating a culture of trust, cooperation, and well-being. In addition to fostering individual success, this fortifies the company overall, enabling it to adjust and prosper in a constantly shifting environment.

3.2.1. Long-Term Implications of Unaddressed Stress

For both people and organizations, ignoring the psychological impacts of job instability can have serious and long-lasting repercussions. Long-term employment uncertainty can cause chronic stress and anxiety in people, which can have a serious negative influence on their physical and mental well-being. Chronic stress has been associated with major health problems such high blood pressure, gastrointestinal ailments, and cardiovascular disease. People who are always worried are more prone to disease and have a harder time recovering from health issues because their immune systems are weakened. Untreated psychological stress can also result in chronic mental health issues including burnout, depression, and anxiety disorders, which further impair a person's quality of life and coping mechanisms.

Chronic stress can damage relationships and interfere with day-to-day functioning in addition to having negative health effects. People who experience long-term job instability may become agitated, reclusive, or unduly preoccupied with work-related issues, which can affect relationships with friends and family. Job insecurity-related financial hardships might intensify these tensions, resulting in domestic strife and mental stress. Untreated stress can have a cumulative effect over time that weakens a person's resilience, sense of purpose, and capacity to face obstacles in the future.

The consequences of a stressed-out staff are equally worrisome for enterprises. Unresolved job instability frequently causes employees to lose attention, motivation, and engagement, which lowers output and quality of work. As workers take time off to recuperate from physical or mental health conditions or to deal with personal difficulties relating to their work circumstances, chronic stress also raises absenteeism rates. Even if the company has no plans to reduce staff, increased turnover is another frequent result as workers search for more secure employment elsewhere. In addition to costing a lot of money to hire, train, and onboard new staff, this churn also leads in the loss of important talent.

Furthermore, ignoring stress has a negative impact on the larger company culture. A workforce that is fearful and unsure often experiences low morale and diminished confidence in management. The performance and resilience of the company may be further weakened by the demoralizing and disengaged feelings that the remaining staff may have as a result of this unfavorable environment. Addressing these long-term implications requires a proactive and holistic approach from both individuals and organizations. For individuals, adopting stress management strategies, seeking mental health support, and focusing on skill-building can mitigate the personal impact of job insecurity. For organizations, fostering a supportive workplace culture, providing transparent communication, and offering resources such as wellness programs and professional development opportunities can help alleviate stress and reinforce trust. Organizations may safeguard the well-being of their workers and create a more resilient, engaged, and productive workforce by identifying and resolving the long-term impacts of job instability. Both individuals and organizations gain from investing in preventative measures and creating a supportive and trusting atmosphere, which guarantees a sustainable future in a labor market that is becoming more and more dynamic.

3.2.2. Building Resilience in the Workforce

One of the most important ways to lessen the psychological effects of job instability and promote a culture of flexibility and development is to help employees become more resilient. Employees that possess resilience are better able to deal with uncertainty, bounce back from failures, and prosper in a constantly evolving workplace. Building a resilient workforce is a way for businesses to improve overall performance and agility in addition to investing in the well-being of their employees.

Giving staff members access to focused training programs is one of the most important aspects of fostering resilience. Workshops and classes that emphasize problem-solving, emotional intelligence, and flexibility assist people in gaining the abilities necessary to successfully handle change. Employees who receive emotional intelligence training, for example, learn how to control their emotions, appreciate the opinions of others, and interact well in trying circumstances. Training in problem-solving and flexibility empowers employees to take a proactive approach to uncertainty, seeing development prospects and coming up with creative answers to novel problems.

Organizations going through major changes, like digitization or restructuring, are good examples of these strategies in action. A business that is adopting digital transformation may provide change management seminars to help staff members comprehend the rationale for the change, lessen resistance, and be ready for new methods of operation. Furthermore, offering reskilling and upskilling chances guarantees that workers have the hard and soft skills needed for new positions, which lowers anxiety and boosts confidence while negotiating career changes. These programs show that the company appreciates employees' efforts and progress while also preparing them for future challenges.

Creating an atmosphere that encourages candid dialogue and teamwork is another aspect of enhancing resilience. A sense of inclusion and ownership is fostered by encouraging staff members to voice their concerns, pose inquiries, and take part in decision-making. Peer support groups and team-building exercises can improve connections between coworkers and foster a positive work environment where people feel encouraged to tackle problems together. This sense of camaraderie and support is further strengthened by mentoring programs, in which seasoned workers help others during times of uncertainty.

By placing a strong emphasis on wellbeing and work-life balance, organizations may also encourage resilience. Building long-term resilience requires people to manage stress and preserve their general health, which may be achieved through wellness initiatives, flexible work schedules, and access to mental health services. By being composed, focused on finding solutions, and sympathetic in the face of change, leaders that exhibit resilience set a good example for their staff and emphasize the need of flexibility and a development mentality.

Building resilience has advantages for more than just individual workers. During times of disruption, a resilient workforce is better able to welcome innovation, adjust to shifting dynamics in the market, and maintain productivity. These attributes provide a stronger competitive advantage to businesses, make them more agility, and promote staff retention. Employees feel empowered and have a sense of purpose because they know they can adapt to change and thrive in a changing labor market.

In the end, increasing workforce resilience benefits both businesses and employees. Organizations may assist their teams in thriving in the face of uncertainty by making investments in the development of adaptable abilities and cultivating a positive work environment, transforming obstacles into chances for advancement and achievement.

3.2.3. A Call for Comprehensive Support Systems

A comprehensive strategy that unites the efforts of people, organizations, and society at large is required to address the psychological toll of employment instability. Developing systems that promote resilience, flexibility, and well-being during times of uncertainty and transition requires the participation of all of stakeholders. Proactive involvement in professional growth and mental health is crucial at the individual level. To preserve emotional equilibrium, people must prioritize self-care by using techniques such as stress reduction, exercise, and mindfulness. The dedication to lifelong learning and skill development is equally significant. People may more confidently handle changes in the labor market by remaining flexible and consistently improving their abilities. Having strong professional and personal networks also gives you access to career possibilities, mentorship, and a feeling of belonging when things become tough.

On the other hand, organizations have a crucial role to play in creating settings that lessen the detrimental effects of employment instability. The cornerstones of establishing stability and trust in the workplace are open communication, compassionate leadership, and proactive support. Giving workers access to career guidance, reskilling courses, and mental health resources guarantees they have the means to succeed. Businesses may also cultivate an inclusive and collaborative culture where workers feel appreciated and supported, especially in times of transition. Organizations may increase employee retention and satisfaction as well as overall productivity and resilience by making investments in the well-being of their workforce.

To solve the underlying issues of employment insecurity, policymakers and society institutions are equally crucial. Supporting people throughout job changes requires strong safety nets, such as increased unemployment compensation, reasonably priced healthcare, and easily accessible retraining programs. The basis for a more equal labor market is further strengthened by laws that support workplace flexibility, fight discrimination, and encourage fair employment practices. Cultural attitudes may be changed via public campaigns and neighborhood projects that promote career reinvention and de-stigmatize job loss. This will help people see job uncertainty as a chance for personal development rather than a failure.

Through recognition and resolution of the affective difficulties linked to job insecurity, society may develop a workforce that is more robust and flexible. The implementation of proactive measures that support stability, empowerment, and well-being requires cooperation between individuals, organizations, and policymakers. By encouraging confidence and security, this all-encompassing strategy not only helps people but also fortifies economies and institutions, opening the door to a more inclusive and sustainable future. Under this approach, job insecurity is viewed as a manageable concern that can be addressed on all levels with resources, support, and opportunities. A labor market that empowers people, supports the growth of companies, and lays the groundwork for long-term economic and social resilience can be achieved by society working together. The next section looks at proactive strategies for navigating Job security challenges.

Part 2:

Proactive Strategies for Navigating Job Security Challenges

Chapter 4: Building Career Resilience: Key Issues and Concerns

Career resilience has become a crucial ability for workers in all industries in an era characterized by fast technical breakthroughs, globalization, and economic volatility. The capacity to adjust to changes, bounce back from setbacks, and maintain employability in a changing labor market is known as career resilience. The capacity to remain adaptable, learn new things constantly, and maintain strong professional networks has become crucial for long-term success as sectors change and traditional career pathways become less predictable.

4.1. Adaptability

The foundation of professional resilience is adaptability. The capacity to adapt to new positions, sectors, or technological advancements guarantees that people may prosper even when the nature of work changes. In sectors like manufacturing, retail, or media that are going through major changes and where automation and digitalization are redefining old jobs, this ability is especially crucial. Professionals may pivot and take advantage of new trends by being adaptable and viewing uncertainty as an opportunity rather than a threat. Employees who adopt hybrid work patterns or become proficient with new digital technologies, for instance, are frequently in a better position to thrive in changing work settings.

Continuous learning has emerged as a crucial component of career resilience in a world where industrial needs and technology breakthroughs are perpetually shifting. Continuous skill development—whether via formal education, online courses, certifications, or on-the-job training—is necessary to stay relevant. In addition to showcasing their technical expertise, professionals who make a commitment to continual learning also show that they can adapt to changing circumstances and remain competitive. Upskilling in fields like artificial intelligence, data analytics, or soft skills like communication and leadership may extend one's career and lead to new possibilities.

Professional networks, which provide access to myriad opportunities, mentoring, and support, are essential for developing professional resilience. During times of uncertainty or professional change, keeping and growing relationships inside one's business or across multiple professions may be quite beneficial. Additionally, networking fosters chances for cooperation, information exchange, and personal development—all of which support professional resilience. Building and sustaining meaningful professional relationships is now simpler than ever thanks to platforms like LinkedIn, industry conferences, and networking events.

Even though career resilience is crucial, many professionals encounter major obstacles while trying to hone these abilities. Attempts to seek professional development or ongoing learning may be hampered by lack of resources, time restrictions, and financial limits. Individuals may also be unable to embrace flexibility due to personal issues like aversion to change or fear of failing. Systemic obstacles like discrimination or unequal access to opportunities can make resilience-building even more difficult for marginalized groups.

People need to be proactive in their professional growth if they want to achieve career resilience. Essential initial stages include defining clear professional goals, evaluating abilities on a regular basis, and pinpointing opportunities for improvement. The resources and direction required to maintain competitiveness may be obtained by utilizing online learning environments, going to seminars, and looking for mentoring. By providing learning and development opportunities, cultivating inclusive workplace environments, and motivating staff to take advantage of growth chances, organizations may support these initiatives.

Resilience in the workplace is now essential in today's fast-paced and uncertain employment environment. By emphasizing networking, flexibility, and ongoing education, professionals may lay the groundwork for sustained success. In the meanwhile, businesses and legislators need to try to eliminate obstacles and provide conditions that enable people to prosper in a world that is constantly changing. By working together, these initiatives can make career resilience a priority for everyone, which will help people, businesses, and the economy as a whole.

4.2. Adaptability: The Cornerstone of Resilience

A key element of professional resilience is adaptability, which enables people to deal with change in an efficient manner. The key to this flexibility is developing a growth mindset, which holds that aptitudes and skills can be acquired by work and education. When professionals see change as a chance for personal development rather than a danger, they may confidently take on new positions, technology, and sectors.

For instance, numerous employees in the retail and hotel industries switched to positions in e-commerce or delivery services during the COVID-19 epidemic, illustrating flexibility in action. To adopt this attitude, one must be willing to explore new options and let go of preconceived notions about potential job pathways. It is crucial for people to deliberately confront these mental obstacles and exercise flexibility since resistance to change frequently results from self-doubt or fear of the unknown.

Developing flexibility might be difficult, despite its significance. Due to inertia, many professionals oppose change and stick to tried-and-true practices. Moreover, organizational cultures that penalize failure or discourage taking risks might impede flexibility. In inflexible hierarchical businesses, for example, people may be reluctant to attempt new things or provide innovative ideas because they are afraid of making errors.

In order to get beyond these obstacles, people and institutions need to create settings that promote experimentation and education. Setting modest, attainable objectives during times of transition is one personal tactic that can help boost self-esteem and gradually reaffirm the advantages of flexibility.

4.3. Networking: The Value of Professional Relationships

Building professional resilience may be achieved through networking, which links people to resources, information, and support networks. Professional connections may lead to new positions, mentorship, and information about market trends. Bypassing the sometimes intense competition of online job boards, a LinkedIn friend, for instance, may alert someone to a job opportunity or suggest them for a position.

However, a lot of people think that networking is only transactional or inauthentic, which leads to misunderstandings or underutilization. Mutual benefit and sincerity are necessary for establishing lasting work connections. It is possible to efficiently grow one's network by participating in industry events, joining associations for professionals, and interacting with colleagues on social media.

4.4. Challenges in Networking

While networking has numerous advantages, some people may find it daunting and even overwhelming, especially those who consider themselves introverted or who believe they lack meaningful contacts or influence. It might be intimidating to consider striking up a conversation or looking for professional connections, particularly in settings where social dynamics or organizational hierarchy are prevalent. These difficulties are exacerbated by impostor syndrome and cultural issues, which make it more difficult for people to leave their comfort zones. In a worldwide company, for example, a junior employee could be reluctant to contact top management for fear of being fired or viewed as unworthy of attention. Similar to this, dealing with leaders or classmates from diverse cultural backgrounds might be frightening because of possible communication or social norm discrepancies.

Imposter syndrome, which is typified by self-doubt and the conviction that one's accomplishments are inadequate or undeserved, can be a major obstacle to successful networking. People may become reluctant to participate or demonstrate their abilities in professional encounters as a result of this internalized dread. Furthermore, cultural norms that place emphasis on hierarchy or prohibit self-promotion might deter people from starting networking initiatives, especially in companies with multinational or varied workforces.

Professionals who want to overcome these obstacles might approach networking strategically and gradually. The most reasonable approach to gaining the required abilities and boosting confidence is sometimes to start small. A low-pressure setting for networking can be established, for example, by extending an invitation to colleagues in one's department or workplace for informal chats or group discussions. Another helpful way to interact with like-minded people is to join professional associations or networking groups that share your interests, whether they be personal or professional.

Connecting with professionals from different sectors and locations is made easy and accessible by virtual platforms like LinkedIn. Without the immediate demands of face-to-face meetings, these platforms enable people to start discussions, join organizations tailored to their business, share ideas. Over time, people may develop deep connections by participating in virtual events, sending personalized connection requests, and leaving insightful comments on shared material.

Another useful strategy for overcoming networking obstacles is to participate in mentoring programs, which offer a more organized and approachable framework for fostering business contacts. People are frequently paired with seasoned professionals through these programs who can provide guidance, encouragement, and insightful advice. The relationship between a mentor and mentee fosters a secure environment to ask questions, get support, and gain confidence in networking and professional advancement.

For those who struggle with imposter syndrome or cultural barriers, seeking out allies or advocates within their organization can also be helpful. Identifying supportive colleagues or leaders who encourage inclusivity can make the process of networking feel less intimidating. Additionally, participating in workshops or training sessions focused on communication, cultural competence, or self-promotion can help individuals build the skills and confidence needed to network effectively.

By starting with small, manageable steps and leveraging accessible resources, individuals can gradually expand their professional networks and overcome the intimidation associated with networking. Over time, these connections can lead to valuable opportunities, collaborations, and personal growth, reinforcing the importance of investing in relationships within the professional sphere. Organizations, too, play a role in fostering inclusive and supportive networking environments, ensuring that employees from all backgrounds feel empowered to connect and thrive.

4.5. The Intersection of Adaptability, Learning, and Networking

Networking frequently acts as a gateway to new ideas, industry trends, and emerging opportunities, inspiring people to acquire new skills or explore alternative career paths. These new skills, in turn, enhance adaptability, enabling professionals to pivot toward roles or projects that align with evolving market demands. Several components of career resilience—adaptability, continuous learning, and networking—work together to help people navigate a dynamic and constantly changing job market. For instance, consider a marketing professional who attends an industry conference. Through networking with peers and thought leaders, they learn about the growing importance of data analytics in marketing campaigns. Speaking with more seasoned coworkers stimulates their interest and motivates them to learn more about this novel field.

The professional chooses to sign up for an online data analytics certification program after being inspired by the advice and support of their network. Their acquired abilities not only help them adjust to changes in the marketing environment, but they also put them in a position to work in positions that call for analytics knowledge, including data-driven campaign management or digital marketing strategist.

Adaptability serves as a link between opportunity and learning in this context. Professionals may turn the knowledge they get from their networks into concrete measures for job progress by being adaptable and bold. Their ability to adjust guarantees that businesses will continue to be competitive and relevant even if industries change quickly as a result of globalization, technology, or changes in the economy. Constant learning also strengthens this flexibility as learning new things gives people more self-assurance and the tools they need to deal with uncertainty.

Additionally, networking is essential to maintaining a development cycle. People's horizons are expanded and a lifelong learning mentality is fostered via interactions with varied experts who expose them to a variety of viewpoints, resources, and strategies. These relationships frequently result in recommendations, joint initiatives, or mentorship possibilities, all of which may serve as stimulants for one's professional and personal growth. Additionally, having a strong professional network gives people both practical and emotional support, enabling them to move careers with more assurance.

The synergy between adaptability, learning, and networking underscores the importance of embracing all three as part of a comprehensive approach to career resilience. Professionals who actively engage in networking, remain committed to learning, and cultivate a mindset of adaptability are better equipped to seize opportunities, overcome challenges, and thrive in an unpredictable job market. This interconnected framework not only enhances individual success but also contributes to the overall resilience and innovation of the workforce.

4.6. The Role of Organizations in Building Resilient Careers

Organizations are crucial in assisting workers in developing career resilience, which is necessary for long-term organizational agility as well as personal success. Companies may equip their employees to meet the demands of a labor market that is changing quickly by fostering settings that promote development, flexibility, and connections. The organization's ability to innovate, retain talent, and stay competitive is strengthened by this assistance, which also benefits the workers.

Employers may help employees develop professional resilience by providing mentoring programs that pair them with seasoned coworkers who can give support, advice, and information. Employees who have mentors can find possibilities for advancement, gain self-assurance, and acquire the skills necessary to adjust to new responsibilities or obstacles. Pairing junior staff members with more seasoned professionals, for example, may speed up learning and create a sense of community, assisting people in feeling encouraged as they pursue their careers.

Another effective tactic is to promote interdepartmental cooperation. By giving workers the chance to collaborate with coworkers from various teams or departments, companies may introduce them to fresh viewpoints, abilities, and concepts. Employees' professional horizons are expanded by this cooperative approach, which also improves their capacity to adjust to a variety of positions and problems. A tech corporation may, for instance, put in place a rotating program that enables staff members to have expertise in a variety of areas, including marketing, product development, and engineering. Employees have a greater awareness of the organization's general operations and improve their skill sets as a result of this exposure, which makes them more useful team players.

Creating a culture of learning is just as important for developing career resilience. By providing access to seminars, online learning environments, and training courses, organizations may promote lifelong learning. Offering financial aid for degrees or certificates in in-demand disciplines like project management or data analytics might encourage workers to advance their skills and stay competitive. Another way to encourage curiosity and teamwork in the workplace is to arrange internal learning events like knowledge-sharing forums or lunch-and-learns.

Another important component of promoting professional resilience is acknowledging and rewarding actions like networking, learning, and adaptation. The importance of these qualities is reinforced when workers who take the initiative to pick up new skills, welcome change, or form relationships both inside and outside the company are publicly honored. Awards, promotions, and simple acknowledgements during team meetings are just a few examples of the various ways that people may show their appreciation. Employees are more inclined to imitate these behaviors when they witness them being valued and rewarded, which has a cascading effect on the entire business.

A key component of this process is leadership. Teams can be motivated to emulate resilient leaders who exhibit flexibility, place a high value on education, and actively network within the sector. To demonstrate that resilience is a common organizational objective, a leader who freely discusses how they overcame a career change or embraced new technology, for instance, sets a strong example for staff members. Employee trust is further increased and a proactive attitude is promoted when leaders communicate openly about opportunities and challenges.

When career resilience is prioritized, firms gain from a more engaged, creative, and adaptable workforce while also giving individuals the confidence to develop and adapt. Organizations may help people succeed in the present while simultaneously preparing them and the company for future uncertainty by integrating mentoring, teamwork, learning, and recognition into their culture.

4.7. Building a Resilient Workforce

The development of career resilience is equally important for organizations. A resilient workforce is one that is engaged, agile, and ready to face future challenges. By funding initiatives that encourage adaptability, lifelong learning, and networking, businesses can create an atmosphere where workers feel empowered to develop and make meaningful contributions, which in turn boosts organizational agility, spurs innovation, and makes it possible for companies to respond to market changes more effectively. Additionally, a focus on resilience helps recruit and retain top talent because workers are more likely to stick with companies that value their professional growth and well-being.

Resilience is a continuous process that calls for an active and collective approach. This entails individuals taking charge of their own growth by exploring opportunities for growth, accepting change, and forming deep professional connections. It involves cultivating an attitude that sees difficulties as opportunities rather than barriers and being adaptable when needed. For businesses, it entails developing a culture that encourages and rewards resiliency. Access to resources, growth opportunities, and transparent leadership are essential for enabling staff members to acquire the abilities and self-assurance they need to be successful.

People can future-proof their jobs and put themselves in a position to succeed no matter what the future brings by putting resilience first. Employers gain by having a staff that is creative, flexible, and ready for the challenges of the contemporary world. Building professional resilience has benefits that go well beyond short-term setbacks and create the foundation for long-term success in a constantly shifting environment. The long-term advantages—for both individuals and organizations—make the trip to resilience well worth pursuing, even though it may call for work and dedication.

Chapter 5: Creating Multiple Income Streams

5.1. Creating Multiple Income Streams: Building Financial Resilience

In an unpredictable economy, the idea of relying on a single income source is increasingly seen as risky. Creating multiple income streams has emerged as a critical strategy for financial resilience and independence. By diversifying earnings through side hustles, passive income ventures, and entrepreneurial activities, individuals can secure their financial futures while pursuing opportunities that align with their interests and skills. This approach not only mitigates the risks of job loss or economic downturns but also enables personal and professional growth.

5.2. Developing Side Hustles and Freelance Work

Working as a freelancer or starting a side business have grown in popularity as strategies to supplement primary income. These businesses provide a flexible source of income by enabling people to monetize their interests, abilities, or specialized skills. A teacher may coach students online over the weekends, while a graphic designer might work on freelance assignments after work. It is now simpler than ever to connect with clients and customers thanks to platforms like Fiverr, Upwork, and Etsy.

The accessibility and scalability of side gigs are what make them appealing. They are a low-risk way to start accumulating financial stability because many of them demand little initial commitment. It can be difficult to juggle a side business and a full-time job, though. Burnout may result from overworking, and it's important to manage any financial ramifications or possible inconsistencies with an employer's policy. Setting defined limits and emphasizing effective time management are common traits of successful side hustlers.

5.3. The Flexibility of Freelance Work

Another source of income diversification is freelance employment. In contrast to conventional side jobs, freelancing frequently entails using professional knowledge to do projects on a project basis. Often working as independent contractors, writers, developers, consultants, and marketers offer specialized services to several clients. Although freelancing allows you independence and the possibility of large income, it also necessitates self-control, client management abilities, and the capacity to weather times of irregular revenue.

Professionals who want to succeed in freelancing need to have robust networks and portfolios. A strong personal brand, internet channels, and word-of-mouth recommendations may all greatly increase exposure and draw in customers. Expanding their skill sets and investing in ongoing education puts freelancers in a better position to land big-time jobs in cutthroat marketplaces.

5.4. Exploring Passive Income Opportunities

Passive income—earnings that require little to no ongoing effort after an initial investment—provides an appealing way to create long-term financial stability. While passive income often requires significant upfront work, the potential for consistent revenue makes it an attractive option. Popular strategies include investing in dividend-paying stocks, rental properties, or real estate investment trusts (REITs). For example, an individual with a background in finance might create an investment portfolio that generates steady returns over time.

The development of digital goods or services is an additional source of passive income. Products that may be created once and sold again include mobile applications, e-books, stock photos, and online courses. A fitness teacher may, for example, produce a series of exercise videos that can be bought or subscribed to, bringing in money over time with no upkeep. Digital product sales are made easier by platforms like Teachable, Gumroad, and Amazon Kindle Direct Publishing, which increases accessibility to this alternative.

5.5. Challenges of Passive Income

While passive income presents a substantial opportunity for long-term wealth accumulation and financial independence, it is not completely effortless. A significant amount of time, dedication, creativity, and perhaps an initial financial commitment are needed to generate consistent passive income. For instance, developing an online course could seem like a simple method to make money, but it requires perseverance and knowledge because it entails several processes. Significant time and effort are required for target audience research, creating excellent and captivating content, creating the course materials, and establishing an intuitive platform. Managing client inquiries, promoting the course to draw in customers, and providing prompt assistance to guarantee user happiness are also continuing obligations. A competitive market need regular content revisions and marketing initiatives to maintain sales over time.

In a similar vein, other passive income sources like creating an app, releasing an eBook, or operating a dropshipping company need initial work to build a consistent cash stream. Gaining traction and creating a steady revenue stream need tasks like audience interaction, product development, branding, and market research. Even seemingly more hands-off assets, like dividend-paying stocks or rental real estate, have their own set of difficulties. While real estate holdings require upkeep, tenant management, and the capacity to handle unforeseen problems like repairs or vacancies, stock investments necessitate careful portfolio management and continual market trend monitoring.

Another important factor to take into account while looking for passive income sources is financial risk. There is an inherent risk of loss whether investing in stocks, real estate, or digital goods. For example, market volatility, recessions, or bad investment decisions can all have an impact on a stock portfolio. Property prices might drop, rental markets can change, and unanticipated costs like repairs or legal issues can reduce earnings in the real estate industry. Due to oversaturation, low demand, or poor marketing tactics, digital products—like applications or online courses—may not be commercially successful. These dangers highlight how crucial it is to tackle passive income projects with thorough preparation and flexibility.

Diversification, realistic return expectations, and in-depth market analysis are all components of a smart passive income strategy. The likelihood of success may be considerably increased by comprehending the target market, researching rivals, and spotting market gaps. By distributing exposure across several sources, diversifying revenue streams—for example, by mixing digital goods with stock or real estate investments—helps reduce risk. Because passive income usually develops gradually rather than offering instant cash rewards, reasonable expectations are just as crucial. In the beginning, passive income must be seen as an addition to active income, with the possibility of developing into a sizable source of income in the future.

Despite the challenges, the rewards of passive income can be substantial. Once established, it offers the opportunity for financial stability, greater flexibility, and the freedom to focus on personal goals or other ventures. By acknowledging the effort and risks involved, aspiring passive income earners can set themselves up for long-term success, turning their initial investments of time and resources into a sustainable financial foundation.

5.6. Entrepreneurial Ventures: Transforming Skills into a Business

Entrepreneurial endeavors provide people an opportunity to turn their knowledge, interests, or original concepts into successful companies. Professionals may exercise creativity, forge their own paths, and take control of their financial and professional destiny through these endeavors. Starting a consultancy, for example, allows people to provide specialized guidance and solutions in fields like management, IT, marketing, and human resources. Consultants may establish themselves as reliable professionals who provide their clients with specialized value by utilizing their networks and industry knowledge.

Similarly, creative entrepreneurs might channel their talents into businesses that reflect their artistic vision. A skilled craftsperson could launch a business producing handmade goods, such as jewelry, ceramics, or home decor, selling them through platforms like Etsy or their own website. Photographers might offer services for weddings, events, or corporate clients, while designers could establish studios to provide branding, graphic design, or digital marketing solutions. These ventures often allow creatives to monetize their passions while building meaningful connections with their customers and communities.

5.6.1. The Potential of Entrepreneurship

Being an entrepreneur may lead to both personal fulfillment and substantial financial benefits. Being self-employed gives entrepreneurs the freedom to create their own projects, establish their own hours, and match their work to their beliefs and objectives. Building a business from the ground up may provide a tremendous sense of satisfaction, especially if it leads to favorable customer reviews, financial success, or the capacity to significantly influence a community or sector. Additionally, as they hone their leadership, problem-solving, and resiliency abilities, entrepreneurs frequently undergo personal growth.

5.6.2. The Challenges of Entrepreneurship

However becoming an entrepreneur is not without its difficulties. Managing funds, establishing and preserving connections with customers, and competing in sometimes crowded marketplaces are just a few of the complicated duties that entrepreneurs must do. A marketing consultant moving from a corporate position to self-employment, for instance, may encounter a number of challenges. Without a strong personal brand or established network, it might be challenging to find early clients. It might be difficult to set competitive pricing in a field with a wide range of rivals as it necessitates meticulous evaluation of the value offered and in-depth market research. Another crucial concern is maintaining steady revenue since project fluctuations, especially in the early phases of a corporation, can cause financial instability.

Entrepreneurs in creative fields face similar obstacles. A photographer, for instance, may struggle to stand out in a competitive market or secure steady bookings. Creatives producing handmade goods might encounter challenges in sourcing quality materials, scaling production, or pricing their products to reflect both value and affordability. Additionally, all entrepreneurs must manage administrative tasks, such as accounting, legal compliance, and marketing, which can be time-consuming and detract from the core focus of their business.

5.7. Strategies for Success

People require a combination of strategic preparation, flexibility, and persistence to be successful in their entrepreneurial endeavors. Identifying demand, target markets, and competitive gaps through in-depth market research is the first step in creating a solid company foundation. Entrepreneurs may access a wider audience by utilizing digital tools and platforms, such as professional networking sites, e-commerce platforms, and social media marketing. Establishing a strong support system with colleagues in the sector, mentors, and partners may also offer helpful advice and development possibilities.

Another essential component of long-term success is sound financial management. To reduce risks and guarantee stability, entrepreneurs should create clear budgets, keep emergency money on hand, and investigate a variety of revenue sources. Seeking experienced guidance from accountants, business coaches, or legal professionals may assist those new to self-employment overcome unknown obstacles and steer clear of expensive blunders.

Achieving financial freedom and personal fulfillment via entrepreneurship requires perseverance, hard effort, and smart thinking. Aspiring entrepreneurs may transform their interests and skills into successful, long-lasting companies by acknowledging and resolving the dangers and difficulties that come with starting their own firm.

5.8. Scaling a Business

One of the most thrilling benefits of becoming an entrepreneur is the possibility of scalability, or expanding a firm beyond its original boundaries and attaining unprecedented levels of success. By broadening their product or service offerings, entering new markets, or growing their operations, entrepreneurs may raise their income and market share by scaling. Effective scaling turns a modest firm into a flourishing enterprise with more financial benefits and a wider influence. To guarantee sustainable growth, the process necessitates strategic decision-making, resource management, and meticulous planning.

5.8.1. Opportunities in Scaling

Depending on the type of business, scaling may take many different shapes. A freelance writer who has established a solid clientele, for instance, may decide to engage younger writers or subcontractors to take on more work, moving into an agency model that can manage bigger projects or service more clients at once. In a similar vein, a neighborhood bakery that has built a devoted clientele may decide to create other sites or begin supplying grocery stores and coffee shops in bulk, greatly increasing its market reach.

Another popular scaling method is launching new goods or services to appeal to a wider market or satisfy changing consumer demands. For example, a small software business may start off with just one application before adding subscription-based services or supplementary tools to its portfolio. Expanding into new markets, whether they be demographic or geographic, is another effective strategy for growing. Using e-commerce platforms to reach new client segments, a local firm may begin selling online in order to reach a national or worldwide audience.

Scalability is made possible by technology and automation. Businesses can cope with rising demand without overworking employees by putting in place solutions like automated marketing platforms, inventory management software, and customer relationship management (CRM) systems. Simplified operations create the groundwork for long-term success by increasing customer satisfaction and efficiency.

5.8.2. Challenges of Scaling

Scaling has many advantages, but it also presents a unique set of difficulties. If rapid expansion is not carefully managed, it can put a pressure on infrastructure, personnel, and financial resources. Overstaffing can result in missed deadlines or worse quality, while recruiting too many people too soon might cause cash flow problems. Similar to this, a company may encounter unanticipated logistical, legal, or cultural obstacles if it enters new areas without conducting sufficient study.

Operational inefficiencies often become more pronounced as a business grows. Processes that worked well for a small operation may no longer be effective at scale, leading to bottlenecks and reduced productivity. Entrepreneurs must be prepared to revisit and refine workflows, invest in new technologies, and sometimes delegate decision-making to ensure the business can handle increased complexity.

Another crucial issue during times of fast expansion is preserving the corporate culture and customer happiness. Maintaining the close-knit relationships and individualized service that may have been essential to the company's early success becomes more difficult as teams and operations increase. To maintain the reputation and values of their business, entrepreneurs must place a high priority on quality assurance, employee involvement, and clear communication.

5.8.3. Strategies for Effective Scaling

Scaling successfully begins with a strong base. With methods and procedures in place that can accommodate expansion without compromising effectiveness or quality, entrepreneurs should make sure their company model is scalable. Before putting any scaling plan into action, it is crucial to do market research to find opportunities and possible hazards. As expansion frequently necessitates an upfront investment in personnel, equipment, or marketing, financial planning is equally crucial.

Creating a solid team is also essential to long-term growth. Employing qualified workers who share the company's goals and values and giving them the tools and training they need to succeed should be the main priority of entrepreneurs. By assigning tasks and giving team members decision-making authority, leadership can concentrate on strategic expansion rather than daily management.

Continuous innovation is another key to scaling. Businesses that regularly assess and adapt to market trends are better positioned to identify new opportunities and stay ahead of competitors. Gathering customer feedback and monitoring industry developments can inform decisions about product expansion, marketing strategies, and operational improvements.

5.8.4. The Long-Term Vision

Growing a company is both an opportunity and a task that calls for striking a careful balance between aspiration and pragmatism. Scaling may result in more impact, more money, and a better market presence when done carefully. Strategic planning, resource management, and a dedication to upholding the principles and standards that characterized the company's early success are necessary, nevertheless. In order to ensure long-term development and resilience in a cutthroat industry, entrepreneurs who adopt these concepts may scale their businesses sustainably.

5.9. Balancing Multiple Income Streams

Managing several sources of income is a great method to lower financial risk and increase wealth, but in order to be sustainable and effective, it has to be well planned, prioritized, and organized. By lowering reliance on a single source of income, diversifying earnings can offer stability; yet, if not handled carefully, balancing several streams of revenue can also result in overstretching and inefficiencies. To be successful, strategies and techniques that optimize the value of each source of revenue must be employed to keep things in balance, and streamline operations.

5.9.1. The Benefits and Challenges of Diversification

There are several benefits to diversifying your sources of income, including increased financial stability, the possibility of earning more money overall, and flexibility in dealing with changes in the economy. A person who has a modest e-commerce firm, a rental property, and a full-time job, for example, is better protected against losing money from any one source. Nonetheless, overseeing a variety of endeavors might present considerable difficulties. Without the right procedures in place, people run the danger of overcommitting themselves, which can result in burnout or the neglect of one or more sources of income.

5.9.2. Tools for Effective Management

Leveraging tools and technology is crucial for efficiently managing different revenue streams. Calendars, project tracking software, and task management applications are examples of time management tools that may assist people in setting priorities, scheduling their activities, and meeting deadlines. Another essential tool that gives a clear picture of cash flow, spending, and savings across revenue streams is budgeting software. People are better able to deploy resources and maintain the financial stability of each endeavor because to this visibility.

Establishing specific financial objectives is equally crucial. People may maintain focus and make wise choices about how to spend their time and money by setting clear goals, such as saving for a down payment on a home, financing a company development, or reaching a particular amount of passive income. These objectives also serve as a standard by which to measure the success of every source of revenue, assisting in determining which projects merit more funding and which could require a reassessment.

5.9.3. Maintaining Realistic Expectations

To prevent burnout and guarantee ongoing progress, it is essential to set reasonable expectations. Understanding that not all sources of income will always function similarly aids people in remaining flexible and preventing needless stress. For instance, seasonal variations in sales may be seen by an e-commerce company, and periods of vacancy may occasionally occur in rental properties. A buffer during slower times may be created by carefully planning for these factors through budgeting and emergency savings.

Last but not least, long-term success depends on preserving equilibrium. Exhaustion and decreased productivity might result from overcommitting to revenue-generating tasks. Establishing limits, such as certain work hours for side projects or frequent downtime, guarantees that people can refuel and stay focused. Assessing each revenue stream's sustainability and performance on a regular basis also aids in finding areas where efforts may be maximized.

Taking care of several sources of money is a rewarding yet challenging task. Through the utilization of time management tools, budgeting software, automation, and task outsourcing as required, people may optimize their financial well-being and successfully balance their endeavors. Long-term success requires prioritizing work-life balance, setting clear objectives, and keeping expectations reasonable. Diversifying income sources may offer flexibility, financial security, and the groundwork for accomplishing more general personal and professional objectives when done correctly.

5.9.4. Leveraging Technology for Income Diversification

Creating and managing various revenue sources is now easier than ever thanks to technology. Digital platforms allow people to promote items, automate company processes, and establish connections with customers. For instance, producers may make money off of their work through sponsorships and ad income on social media sites like Instagram and TikTok. In a similar vein, online store setup and operation are made easier by programs like Shopify and WooCommerce.

Additionally, technology makes passive income possible through systems like affiliate marketing, which allow users to promote third-party items and receive commissions. A travel-related blogger may, for instance, connect to websites that book flights or hotels in order to get affiliate revenue. Over time, these possibilities can yield significant profits, but they also demand persistent work and smart strategy. For instance, a teacher who adapts to the demand for virtual education might create an online tutoring service, combining their existing expertise with a willingness to embrace digital tools. This approach not only enhances earning potential but also fosters resilience in a rapidly changing economic landscape.

Having a growth-oriented attitude is crucial for creating and sustaining different revenue sources. To successfully navigate the complexity of diversification, one must be willing to develop new abilities and see obstacles as opportunities. Professionals that value flexibility and creativity are more likely to spot and seize new possibilities, whether they arise in internet platforms, freelancing marketplaces, or business endeavors.

As the labor market continues to be shaped by economic uncertainty, the significance of diversifying sources of income is expected to increase. Entrepreneurship, passive income, and freelancing are avenues for achieving personal development, professional freedom, and financial independence. Through the use of technology, proactive thinking, and prudent resource management, people may create diversified income portfolios that help them achieve their objectives and offer stability in an uncertain environment. Ultimately, careful preparation, persistent work, and flexibility are the keys to successful income diversification. Creating various revenue streams becomes a potent tool for reaching both financial and personal fulfillment when these conditions are met.

Chapter 6: Taking Control of Your Finances

6.1. Taking Control of Your Finances: A Foundation for Security and Growth

The foundation of personal well-being is financial stability, which affects not only material security but also emotional and mental health. However, for many people, effectively managing finances can be a major challenge, frequently resulting in stress, anxiety, and missed opportunities for growth. Taking charge of your finances is about more than just making ends meet; it's about building a solid foundation for long-term security, achieving peace of mind, and unlocking the freedom to pursue your goals without constant financial worry. To achieve this, you must be intentional, disciplined, and dedicated to putting important strategies like emergency fund building, debt management, and living within your means into practice.

6.1.1. Building an Emergency Fund

Creating an emergency fund is one of the most important steps toward financial stability. As a safety net for finances, an emergency fund acts as a buffer against unforeseen costs like auto repairs, medical expenditures, or job loss. People are frequently compelled to use high-interest credit cards or loans in the absence of such a fund, which can make financial problems worse. Three to six months' worth of living expenditures should be saved in a conveniently accessible account, according to experts. This goal may be made more attainable by starting small, such setting aside a portion of each paycheck. Knowing that you have a safety net for life's unforeseen events might eventually ease financial strain and enhance general wellbeing.

6.1.2. Managing Debt Wisely

One typical barrier to financial stability is debt, which must be managed well in order to build a sustainable financial future. Financial hardship may be considerably decreased by being aware of the terms of your commitments and setting payback priorities, regardless of whether you have a mortgage, school loans, or credit card debt. The debt snowball technique is a well-liked strategy in which people prioritize paying off minor debts to gain momentum before taking on larger ones. As an alternative, the debt avalanche strategy reduces long-term expenses by giving priority to loans with the highest interest rates. Repayment management can also be improved by refinancing high-interest debts or combining loans into a lower-interest choice. Above all, avoiding needless debt and developing the ability to discriminate between requirements and wants are critical behaviors for preserving financial stability.

6.1.3. Living Within Your Means

A key component of financial stability is living within one's means, yet many people struggle to do so because of advertising, social pressures, or bad money management practices. This strategy entails setting saving above enjoyment and balancing your income and expenses. A useful technique to attain this balance is making a budget, which keeps track of earnings, expenditures, and savings objectives. Classifying spending and identifying opportunities for cost-cutting is now easier than ever thanks to modern budgeting tools and applications. It's crucial to develop attention about purchases and learn to distinguish between necessary and frivolous expenditure. Savings may be made a priority rather than an afterthought by using a "pay yourself first" strategy, which treats savings as a fixed expenditure and not an afterthought.

6.1.4. Reducing Financial Stress and Building a Path to Stability

People may greatly lessen their financial stress by focusing on five fundamental techniques: controlling debt, saving for emergencies, and living within their means. Knowing that your finances are in order gives you a sense of control that not only improves your peace of mind but also puts you in a better position to face unforeseen obstacles head-on. Furthermore, possibilities to pursue long-term objectives like house ownership, company startup, or retirement investment are made possible by financial stability.

6.2. Looking Beyond the Basics

Reaching financial stability is only the first step. People may concentrate on increasing their wealth through investments, passive income sources, or other financial vehicles after the fundamentals are in place. Gaining knowledge of financial concepts like risk management, tax planning, and compound interest may lead to more chances for security and advancement. Customized advice for creating a sustainable financial future may be obtained by speaking with a financial counselor or by using online financial planning tools.

6.2.1. Emergency Funds: A Lifeline in Uncertain Times

An emergency fund is an essential safety net for finances that is intended to shield people from unforeseen costs like unanticipated medical bills, auto repairs, or an abrupt loss of employment. Because life is unpredictable, unanticipated expenses can occur at any time, and even the most meticulously prepared budgets can become unstable if proper planning isn't done. People may rest easy knowing they have a safety net to handle unforeseen circumstances without jeopardizing their long-term financial objectives by putting away money expressly for emergencies. Every financial expert advises having an emergency fund that can cover three to six months' worth of necessities, including rent, utilities, groceries, and medical care.

The primary purpose of an emergency fund is to reduce reliance on high-interest credit options during crises. In situations where quick cash is needed, many turn to credit cards or payday loans, which often come with exorbitant interest rates that can snowball into unmanageable debt. By having a dedicated reserve of emergency savings, individuals can address unexpected costs without incurring additional financial burdens. For instance, a sudden medical expense or major home repair can be paid directly from the emergency fund, saving the individual from paying interest on borrowed money. This proactive approach not only alleviates immediate stress but also minimizes long-term financial strain.

One of the biggest interruptions that an emergency fund may lessen is losing one's job. It may be disastrous to lose a reliable source of money, especially if monthly expenses and family obligations continue. During the changeover, an emergency fund serves as a vital link, paying for necessities like groceries, electricity, and rent while the person looks for new work. In contrast to someone who is rushing to obtain loans or borrow from friends and family, someone who has saved enough to support their household for several months may feel more confident and focused throughout the job search. Instead of making snap decisions out of desperation, this financial buffer enables careful decision-making.

Although creating an emergency fund takes time and work, the rewards are well worth the effort. The wisest course of action is frequently to start small, especially for people with little extra money to spend. Over time, putting aside even a small amount from each paycheck might add up to a sizable investment. Making saving a habit and streamlining the procedure are two benefits of automating payments to a specific savings account. Progress can also be accelerated by directing unforeseen windfalls, such tax returns, bonuses, or cash gifts, straight to the emergency fund. These modest, regular steps guarantee that the money increases gradually without having a big influence on daily finances.

Despite its significance, many people put off creating an emergency fund because they have conflicting financial goals or believe that conserving money necessitates substantial contributions. But in an emergency, even small savings may make a big difference. Viewing the fund as a long-term commitment rather than a one-time endeavor is crucial. In addition to protecting their financial security, those who prioritize emergency savings also cultivate a sense of security and control over their life. In the end, an emergency fund is more than just cash on hand; it serves as a buffer against life's unforeseen events and a starting point for constructing financial resilience.

6.2.2. Challenges in Building Emergency Funds

Building an emergency fund is crucial, but it may be difficult, especially for those who are living paycheck to paycheck. Setting aside money for an emergency fund can sometimes be challenging due to conflicting financial commitments, such as debt repayment or retirement savings. However, people may progressively create this vital safety net by beginning small and allocating even a tiny amount of each paycheck.

One good technique is to automate saves. People may prioritize their emergency fund without having to think about it by establishing automated payments to a specific savings account. Additionally, development may be accelerated by boosting the fund with windfalls like bonuses or tax returns.

6.2.3. Debt Management: Reducing Financial Strain

The foundation of financial control is debt management, which helps people reestablish stability and concentrate on their long-term financial objectives. Credit card balances, payday loans, and personal loans are examples of high-interest debt that may easily become out of hand if left unchecked. This can lead to a vicious cycle of financial stress and restrict one's capacity to save or invest for the future. Because interest rates compound, it can be difficult to pay off debt after it has accrued, and people frequently end up paying much more over time than they initially borrowed. In addition to relieving immediate financial strain, efficient debt management releases funds for reaching more general financial goals, such retirement savings or emergency fund building.

The debt snowball strategy, which emphasizes paying off lesser debts first to generate momentum, is one of the most popular debt repayment tactics. This strategy places a strong emphasis on psychological gains since paying off lesser sums gives one a sense of achievement and inspires them to take on bigger obligations. If someone has several credit card balances, for instance, they could focus on paying off the one with the lowest balance first while only making the minimum payments on the others. They create a "snowball effect" that increases with each succeeding payments by rerouting the payment amount from the smallest debt to the next smallest balance.

A more scientific approach is used by the debt avalanche technique, which prioritizes loans with the highest interest rates in order to reduce overall expenses. By starting with the most costly loans, this strategy aims to gradually lower the overall amount paid. The avalanche approach, for example, would transfer more payments to the higher-interest credit card while maintaining minimum payments on lower-interest bills if a person had two credit cards, one with a 15% interest rate and the other with a 25% rate. This strategy is especially useful for people who want to save money over time, even if it could take longer to see benefits than the snowball method.

Whatever the approach, having a thorough awareness of one's financial responsibilities is essential for effective debt management. This entails being aware of each debt's balance, interest rate, and terms of repayment. Spreadsheets, budgeting applications, and expert financial guidance are some examples of tools that may assist people in organizing their debts and developing a sensible payback schedule. Whether using an avalanche, snowball, or hybrid strategy, people may progressively lessen their financial load, recover control over their resources, and clear the path to financial stability and independence by being disciplined and dedicated to their chosen course of action.

6.2.4. Barriers to Effective Debt Management

It may be quite difficult to manage debt, particularly for people with large financial commitments or little income. Many people find it difficult to make extra contributions to lower principal amounts, much alone to meet minimum payments. In these situations, getting expert guidance from credit counselors or looking at alternatives like debt consolidation might be helpful.

While paying off current debt, it's crucial to refrain from taking on additional debt. This calls for a dedication to living within one's means and avoiding the temptation to use credit to pay for luxuries. Making sure that debt repayment stays a top priority during this process may be greatly aided by a well-structured budget. An essential component of financial control is living within one's means. It entails putting needs before wants and making sure that spending doesn't outpace income. This necessitates making a distinction between necessities like food and accommodation and discretionary expenses like entertainment or eating out. A sustainable financial plan may be made by people by concentrating on their requirements and minimizing wasteful spending.

A person making $4,000 a month, for instance, may set aside 50% of their income for needs, 30% for discretionary expenditure, and 20% for debt reduction and savings. Often known as the 50/30/20 rule, this strategy offers a well-rounded structure for money management that nevertheless permits flexibility and leisure.

One effective strategy for living within one's means is budgeting. People can find areas where they could be overspending and make changes to better fit their financial objectives by keeping track of their income and expenses. A person who observes a trend of often ordering takeout, for example, can decide to cook more frequently and redirect the money toward debt repayment or savings. Budgeting is now easier than ever thanks to modern technologies. Applications such as Mint, YNAB (You Need a Budget), and PocketGuard provide easy-to-use tools for goal-setting, spending tracking, and progress tracking. People may use these tools to make wise financial decisions and maintain accountability.

6.3. Overcoming Challenges to Living Within Means

Living within one's means might be especially difficult in a culture that values quick satisfaction and materialism. Overspending can be tempted by advertising, social pressures, and the convenience of internet buying. However, people may avoid these temptations and maintain focus on their financial objectives by practicing self-discipline and awareness. Adopting a delayed gratification mentality is one tactic. People might consider if an item fits with their aims or if they would be better off spending their money elsewhere before making non-essential purchases. Positive habits can also be strengthened by establishing clear financial objectives and acknowledging little accomplishments.

6.4. The Long-Term Benefits of Financial Control

Financial stability is only one of the long-term advantages of taking charge of your money via sustainable budgeting, debt management, and emergency reserves. Among the benefits are decreased stress, enhanced relationships, and more freedom to pursue personal as well as professional goals. For instance, someone who has a sizable emergency fund and no debt may feel more comfortable changing careers or launching their own company. Additionally, having financial control offers comfort and a sense of empowerment. People may concentrate on other aspects of life, such as personal development and family and community participation, when they know that their finances are in order. The whole quality of life may be greatly improved by taking a comprehensive approach to financial well-being.

6.5. Conclusion

Managing your money is a continuous process that calls for self-control, preparation, and flexibility. People may lay a solid basis for financial stability and independence by living within their means, managing their debt well, and setting aside money for emergencies. In addition to easing short-term financial burden, these strategies open the door to long-term prosperity and adaptability in a constantly shifting economic environment. Consistent work and deliberate choices make financial control a way of life rather than just a goal.

Part 3: Coping with Redundancy and Finding Fulfillment

Chapter 7: Managing Emotional Fallout

7.1. Managing Emotional Fallout: Navigating the Challenges of Redundancy

One of the most emotionally taxing situations a person may go through is losing their job or being laid off, which can affect many facets of their lives. As occupations are closely linked to how individuals see themselves and their roles in society, losing a job frequently has an impact on a person's sense of identity and self-worth in addition to the immediate disturbance to financial security. It might cause emotions of inadequacy or worry about the future since it can feel like you're losing a piece of who you are. The abrupt shift in habit and the need to rethink long-term goals can leave people feeling vulnerable and disoriented, which adds to the emotional toll.

Losing a job may have a variety of emotional effects, and it's normal for people to feel a wide range of strong emotions. Significant anxiety might be brought on by worries about one's financial stability, fear of the future, or uncertainty about obtaining new work. Although melancholy at the loss of purpose or the companionship of a job might result in feelings of loneliness, anger may also surface, directed toward situations, bosses, or even oneself. These feelings frequently happen at the same time or fluctuate erratically, which exacerbates the feeling of overload.

Effectively controlling these feelings is essential to reestablishing equilibrium and continuing on after such a major upheaval. Since repressing emotions might result in further stress or emotional tiredness, it is crucial to first recognize and acknowledge the emotions that surface. Speaking candidly about these emotions with dependable family members, friends, or licensed counselors can aid in processing the event and gaining perspective. Support networks are extremely helpful during this period, providing both practical guidance for adjusting to the change and emotional support.

Another crucial element of coping with the difficulties of losing a job is putting self-care first. Keeping up a healthy regimen that include regular exercise, well-balanced meals, and enough sleep will assist maintain emotional stability and give you the energy you need to face the future. Maintaining well-being may also be greatly aided by pursuits like writing, meditation, and hobbies that foster mental clarity and relaxation.

Losing a job can have an enormous emotional impact, but it can also be a chance to think and consider other options. This time of uncertainty may be turned into an opportunity for personal development and reinvention by taking the time to assess one's interests, abilities, and professional objectives. Seeking out professional guidance, such as career counseling or job placement services, can provide direction and build confidence in moving toward new opportunities.

Recovering from a job loss is ultimately a very personal process that calls for perseverance and patience. People may go through this trying time and come out on the other side with fresh purpose and clarity if they acknowledge the emotional difficulties, look for assistance, and prioritize taking care of themselves. Even while the voyage might be intimidating, it offers the opportunity to rethink one's future and forge a fresh route to contentment and security.

7.2. Acceptance: Acknowledging Feelings Without Judgment

Managing the emotional fallout of redundancy begins with practicing acceptance, an important but often-overlooked aspect of the healing process. Redundancy usually sets off a cascade of emotions, from sadness over the loss of opportunities or routines to anger over perceived injustices and fear and uncertainty about the future. While these feelings can be overwhelming, recognizing and accepting them without passing judgment is a powerful way to start moving forward. While denying or suppressing emotions may provide short-term respite, it often causes the emotional recovery process to drag on.

The first step in acknowledging emotions is realizing that experiencing a range of contradictory feelings to redundancy is natural. It's normal to be afraid of the unknown, including worries about the security of your finances or finding a new career. Anger might be directed toward oneself, the employer, or the events that led to the layoff. When people lament the loss of their professional identities, daily routines, and connections at work, sadness and grief frequently appear. Even if they are unpleasant, these emotions are real and should be dealt with.

To practice acceptance, one must also be aware of the outside influences that frequently result in redundancy. For example, a person who loses their job may at first feel guilty or blame themselves for their poor performance. But acknowledging that redundancy is often the consequence of outside factors—like market demand changes, firm reorganizations, or economic downturns—can help reframe the experience. This viewpoint lessens emotions of failure on a personal level and promotes a more positive outlook for taking on the next challenges.

One of the most important aspects of acceptance is providing channels for emotional expression. Journaling offers a secure environment for people to analyze their experiences and is a useful tool for structuring ideas and examining emotions. Clarity and insightful realizations might result from putting certain worries, annoyances, or hopes in writing. In a similar vein, speaking with a counselor, family member, or trusted friend provides a chance to express feelings and get perspective. People might feel less alone by having these discussions, which can offer consolation as well as support and useful guidance.

Acceptance is the recognition of the existing state as a place to begin the process of healing and development, not resignation. It enables people to face their emotions head-on, pinpoint the things they can control, and start imagining a future. Redundancy survivors may create the groundwork for resilience and eventually discover new chances for success and fulfillment by dealing with the emotional consequences with candor and self-compassion.

7.3. Overcoming the Fear of Vulnerability

Overcoming a deeply rooted fear of vulnerability is frequently necessary in order to acknowledge feelings. It can be difficult for people to publicly acknowledge feelings of grief, anxiety, or uncertainty after losing their job because success is often strongly associated with the appearance of strength and perseverance in many communities. Despite their internal struggles, people may repress their feelings or put up a brave front as a result of this social pressure. However, a crucial first step on the path to acceptance and healing is realizing that these feelings are a normal and acceptable reaction to big life events.

It may be liberating to see vulnerability as a strength instead of a weakness. It takes guts to acknowledge to oneself and others that quitting a job is unpleasant, frightening, or confusing. Being vulnerable enables people to deal with their feelings in a genuine way, which promotes emotional development and resilience. People can become more self-aware, recognize their needs, and start to reestablish a sense of purpose via this openness. Reminding people that they are not alone in their experiences and fostering meaningful connections can also result from sharing these feelings with family, support groups, or trusted friends.

In addition to embracing vulnerability, practicing mindfulness or meditation can further support the process of acceptance. These techniques are powerful tools for grounding individuals in the present moment, especially during times of uncertainty and upheaval. Mindfulness encourages nonjudgmental awareness of thoughts and feelings, allowing individuals to observe their emotions without being overwhelmed or consumed by them. For example, instead of dwelling on fears about the future or regrets about the past, mindfulness helps individuals focus on what they can control in the here and now.

Even brief meditation sessions might help bring clarity and serenity among the emotional upheaval of losing a job. Methods like body scans, guided visualizations, and deep breathing can assist people in controlling their stress reactions and gaining a more impartial view of their situation. Regular mindfulness practice can eventually increase emotional resilience, empowering people to face difficulties with composure and self-compassion. This combination of acknowledging emotions and cultivating mindfulness can lay the foundation for a healthier relationship with one's feelings. People can gain the clarity and strength necessary to move forward by facing their fears, accepting vulnerability, and practicing present-moment awareness. These techniques not only encourage acceptance but also enable people to rebuild their lives with purpose and confidence when faced with redundancy or job loss.

7.4. Support Systems: The Importance of Connection

Support networks are a vital lifeline during emotionally turbulent times, providing consolation, perspective, and encouragement when needed most. Our relationships with others, whether they be with friends, family, or licensed counselors, offer a vital basis for overcoming difficult circumstances like layoffs or job loss. In addition to reducing feelings of loneliness, these connections provide doors for deep discussions that may result in revelations, answers, and a revitalized sense of direction.

When it comes to offering emotional support, friends are frequently crucial. Confiding in a close friend enables people to express their worries, annoyances, and anxieties without fear of criticism. Friends may provide new insights or useful ideas that had not been thought of, making these discussions both instructive and therapeutic. A close friend could, for instance, provide counsel based on their personal experiences with career transitions, suggest networking opportunities, or give useful employment leads. Beyond helpful advice, people can find great relief just by knowing they are not alone in their troubles and that they are being heard and recognized.

In times of uncertainty, family members are also essential in providing stability and confidence. In addition to offering mental stability, a strong family support network may offer useful support like childcare, money, or a temporary place to stay if necessary. Family's familiarity and unwavering affection may serve as a protective barrier against the stress of losing a job, providing a secure and supportive space where people can refocus and recover. Family members frequently serve as a reminder of a person's perseverance and abilities, which strengthens the conviction that one can overcome obstacles.

Seeking advice from a qualified counselor or therapist can be very helpful for people who feel particularly overwhelmed or unsure about how to proceed. These qualified experts offer a private, secure setting where people may examine their feelings, pinpoint triggers, and create useful coping mechanisms. Counselors may assist people in developing resilience, reframing negative ideas, and creating attainable objectives for the future. In order to provide people useful strategies for controlling their anxiety and regaining control, therapists may also recommend cognitive-behavioral therapies, stress-reduction activities, or mindfulness exercises.

Peer groups and community networks are examples of support systems that go beyond interpersonal connections. Participating in online or in-person support groups might help people meet others going through similar struggles. While the group's encouragement and collective expertise can inspire fresh methods to problem-solving, sharing experiences within these groups promotes understanding and friendship. Making connections with colleagues who have handled layoffs or job changes well can also yield insightful information and inspiration.

Recovery and growth depend on the integration of support networks into the process of handling emotional turmoil. These relationships provide the comfort and resources needed to get through difficult situations, whether it's asking friends for help, finding comfort in family ties, or seeking the counsel of a professional. People may gain insight, strengthen their resilience, and take significant action toward a more promising and secure future by utilizing the strength of these networks.

7.5. Building a Network of Support

Support groups and community networks, in addition to personal relationships, are essential in assisting people in overcoming the difficulties associated with job loss or layoff. These groups, which are frequently accessible in cities or online, offer a friendly environment for others going through comparable situations to connect, exchange stories, and encourage one another. Groups created especially for those coping with unemployment or professional transitions, for example, are held in many places and provide both emotional support and useful tools. In addition to promoting a sense of camaraderie, these environments enable members to share advice on resume writing, job seeking, and interview techniques. It may be quite comforting to know that others are aware of and face comparable difficulties, which lessens feelings of loneliness and fosters hope and solidarity.

These groups provide advantages that go beyond helpful guidance. Making connections with others who have experienced or are presently dealing with redundancy gives them access to a variety of viewpoints and problem-solving techniques. Members frequently relate anecdotes of their own achievements and tenacity, which can encourage and inspire others to maintain hope for their own paths. For instance, learning about someone who discovered a rewarding work after a period of uncertainty or who successfully transferred to a new field may be energizing and insightful. People feel understood and empowered to take proactive efforts toward their objectives in this supportive group that is created by their shared experiences.

During times of job loss, professional networks like LinkedIn or forums tailored to a particular field may also be quite helpful. Even when people are in between employment, these platforms allow them to keep and grow their professional networks. People may remain up to date on industry trends, take part in insightful conversations, and look into possible mentorship possibilities by interacting with their networks. In example, mentors may offer direction and counsel pertaining to a given professional path, assisting people in seeing possibilities and formulating winning plans.

Additionally, professional networks provide access to chances for career exploration and cooperation. To increase their expertise and exposure in their profession, people might, for example, take part in webinars, attend virtual industry events, or join pertinent LinkedIn groups. In addition to keeping people in touch with their industry, these contacts may provide doors to collaborations, freelance work, or employment prospects that would not have otherwise been available. Making connections with experts who are actively working in the sector guarantees that people stay competitive and relevant, even when they are unemployed.

Virtual communities and online forums provide additional avenues for seeking support. Discussions where people may ask for guidance, share their experiences, and find support are held on websites such as Reddit, Meetup, or specialist job forums. People from a variety of backgrounds and experiences frequently congregate in these areas, offering a multitude of tools and insights for individuals managing redundancy. Online platforms' simplicity also makes it simpler for people to get help from any location, extending their reach beyond opportunities in their immediate area.

The experience of losing a job may be turned into an opportunity for development and connection by participating in support groups, professional platforms, and community networks. People may go on with confidence and purpose by using these tools to access possible opportunities, emotional support, and practical counsel. These networks act as a reminder that recovery and regeneration are completely possible with the correct assistance and that no one must deal with redundancy alone.

7.6. Self-Care Practices: Replenishing Energy and Self-Esteem

Redundancy frequently has a negative impact on energy levels and self-esteem, leaving people feeling exhausted and uncertain about their value. Self-care becomes crucial to emotional healing during these periods, acting as a means of reestablishing resilience as well as a healing technique. During a time of turmoil, people can restore stability, confidence, and control by partaking in activities that promote their physical, mental, and emotional well-being. People who prioritize self-care provide the circumstances required for development, clarity, and a revitalized sense of purpose.

One of the best strategies to combat the stress and lack of energy that are frequently associated with redundancy is to engage in physical activity. Walking, yoga, swimming, and cycling are examples of regular activity that not only enhances physical health but also produces endorphins, which are the body's natural mood boosters. These endorphins aid in overcoming depressive or anxious sensations and substituting them with sentiments of serenity and optimism. Exercises that focus on mindfulness and breathe control, like yoga or tai chi, can be particularly helpful since they help people focus and clear their minds. The combination advantages of physical movement and exposure to nature, which have been demonstrated to improve mood and lower stress, may be obtained from even something as basic as going for a daily stroll outside.

Another effective way to take care of oneself is through creative outlets, which enable people to rekindle hobbies that may have been neglected due to the pressures of full-time employment and to constructively channel their emotions. You can feel happy and accomplished when you paint, write, perform music, create, or even garden. Through therapeutic emotional release and a revitalized sense of purpose, these activities allow people to express themselves in ways that words can't always. Writing in a diary, for instance, can assist people in processing their experiences and gaining new perspectives, while painting or playing an instrument offers a contemplative, absorbing diversion from everyday concerns.

Simple, daily routines are also essential for preserving general wellbeing and establishing a feeling of routine in unpredictable times. Keeping a regular sleep cycle ensures that people have the mental and physical capacity to face problems by regulating mood and energy levels. In addition to providing nourishment, cooking and eating nutritious meals creates a tiny but significant pattern that promotes stability. Furthermore, staying hydrated and avoiding drugs like alcohol or caffeine might improve general health by enhancing mood and concentration.

Self-care can also involve cultivating supportive relationships and embracing activities that nurture the soul. Spending time with loved ones, joining community groups, or participating in hobbies that foster connection and collaboration can alleviate feelings of isolation and provide a sense of belonging. Acts of kindness, such as volunteering, not only benefit others but also instill a sense of purpose and fulfillment in those who give their time and energy.

The habit of establishing boundaries to safeguard one's emotional and mental space is equally crucial. This might be turning down obligations that seem too big, setting aside time for introspection, or avoiding people who make stress worse. Developing resilience via self-care is about preparing oneself to meet obstacles with more power and clarity, not about running away from them.

During redundancy, integrating self-care into everyday life is not only a coping mechanism; it is a chance to reevaluate and prioritize what is most important. People may start the healing process, regain their confidence, and create the foundation for a more satisfying future by making investments in activities that promote mental clarity, emotional balance, and physical health. Self-care serves as a reminder to people that their value goes well beyond their position and that taking care of oneself is an essential first step in starting a new chapter full of opportunity and development.

7.7. Rebuilding Confidence Through Self-Care

Maintaining one's physical health is only one aspect of self-care; another is fostering one's sense of self and individuality. Many people have emotions of inadequacy or self-doubt following redundancy. Confidence may be restored by taking the time to acknowledge minor accomplishments, such finishing a job application or updating a CV. A feeling of self-worth can be further strengthened by repeating affirmations or thinking back on prior accomplishments.

Self-care also includes making investments in one's own personal growth. For instance, taking up a hobby, volunteering, or learning a new skill may broaden perspectives and increase confidence. These exercises can assist people in imagining alternative job choices and show that personal development and contentment are achievable even under trying circumstances.

7.7.1. Balancing Rest and Productivity

While self-care frequently highlights the value of rest and relaxation, sustaining emotional health and motivation during times of redundancy requires striking the correct balance between leisure time and meaningful engagement. Although redundancy offers an opportunity for introspection, rejuvenation, and reevaluating life goals, it may also result in emotions of discontent and stagnation in the absence of structure or forward motion. By finding this balance, people may take care of their physical and mental well-being and make significant strides toward their long-term objectives.

Redundancy periods are a great opportunity for reflection and realignment, enabling people the chance to think about their long-term goals, personal beliefs, and professional trajectory. However, positive endeavors, such as networking, skill development, or job seeking, aid in fostering a feeling of achievement and purpose. By breaking down more complex problems into smaller, more manageable steps, setting attainable daily or weekly objectives may offer discipline without becoming overwhelming. These objectives may be reaching out to a professional contact, updating a résumé, attending a workshop, or applying to a certain amount of jobs.

Someone dealing with redundancy, for instance, may spend their mornings engaging in targeted job-search activity. This might entail doing company research, customizing applications, or interview practice. Conversely, afternoons might be set out for self-care activities like working out, reading, or doing creative endeavors. By addressing both professional and personal requirements, this methodical approach helps to preserve equilibrium and productivity.

Another intentional activity that can improve employability and supplement self-care is skill development. Redundancy frequently gives people the time and freedom to develop new interests or hone current abilities. In addition to increasing confidence, taking an online course, going to webinars, or being certified in a high-demand sector shows prospective employers that you are proactive. For example, a marketing professional may enroll in a data analytics course, while an educator might investigate novel approaches in online learning. These initiatives help people improve personally and maintain their competitiveness in their line of work.

Avoiding burnout requires striking a balance between these activities and deliberate leisure. Self-care techniques like mindfulness, meditation, or just taking up a hobby offer much-needed mental clarity and calm. People can rejuvenate during this downtime, giving them the energy and concentration they need to accomplish their daily goals. Incorporating social connection breaks into a well-rounded schedule might involve engaging in community groups or spending time with friends and family.

Maintaining a sense of progress during redundancy not only supports emotional well-being but also builds momentum for the future. It reinforces the belief that even in times of uncertainty, positive steps can be taken toward new opportunities and personal growth. By combining purposeful activity with self-care, individuals can navigate redundancy with resilience, creating a foundation for both immediate stability and long-term success. This balanced approach turns a potentially challenging period into an opportunity for renewal, discovery, and forward movement.

7.7.2. Recognizing the Role of Gratitude

Even during difficult situations like job loss or redundancy, cultivating thankfulness is a potent and transforming self-care technique that may greatly improve emotional well-being. A much-needed sense of balance and hope may be obtained by changing perspective to acknowledge and value the positive aspects of one's life, even if it may be challenging to do so when experiencing feelings of uncertainty and loss. By rephrasing difficulties, gratitude lessens their emotional impact and promotes an optimistic and resilient mindset—two qualities crucial for managing professional changes.

It's easy and beneficial to include thankfulness into everyday activities. Keeping a thankfulness notebook, for example, enables people to consider the good things in their lives, no matter how minor. Whether it's a friend's encouragement, a moment of laughing, or the beauty of a sunrise, writing down three things for which you are grateful each day can help you develop the habit of appreciating the positive even in the face of adversity. In addition to balancing depressing or frustrating emotions, this exercise gradually rewires the brain to automatically focus on good events.

It might also be helpful to set aside even a small amount of time each day to consider appreciation. This can be done as part of a mindfulness exercise, at the conclusion of the day, or at a peaceful time in the morning. A person who has lost their work, for instance, could be thankful for the additional time they have to spend with loved ones, take up an activity they used to like, or concentrate on their own development and well-being. These contemplations serve as a reminder that life still offers opportunities for happiness, connection, and possibility, even in the midst of adversity.

Moreover, gratitude promotes a sense of empowerment by highlighting one's own assets and talents. Acknowledging one's capacity to overcome obstacles, adjust to novel circumstances, or pick up new abilities boosts self-assurance while facing the future. For example, someone can thank oneself for their problem-solving skills or for their ability to bounce back from setbacks, reminding themselves that they have what it takes to get through the challenges they face today.

Sharing appreciation with others may strengthen bonds and increase its beneficial benefits, going beyond personal practice. Telling friends, family, or coworkers how much you appreciate their assistance not only improves relationships but also spreads happiness. Writing a thank-you card or openly praising someone for their effort are examples of acts of kindness that may promote camaraderie and support amongst others.

Being grateful is not the same as denying problems or acting as though they don't exist. Rather, it is about realizing that there are parts of life that offer stability, joy, and significance even in the face of loss and uncertainty. By encouraging emotional resilience, this viewpoint enables people to face professional changes with hope and a fresh sense of direction. People may build a strong emotional foundation, open their eyes to new possibilities, and establish an effective stress-reduction strategy by including thankfulness into their self-care routines.

7.7.3. Balancing Productivity and Leisure

Finding a balance between job and leisure activities is another aspect of leading a fulfilling life. Goal-setting is vital, but so is setting aside time to unwind, think, and enjoy life. Recharging and preserving a sense of wellbeing may be achieved by planning downtime for enjoyable and soothing pursuits like reading, spending time with loved ones, or going on nature hikes.

By striking a balance, burnout is avoided and contentment is guaranteed to come from enjoying ordinary times as well as accomplishments. A person pursuing a professional certification, for instance, may strike a balance between their job and regular family time or walks, resulting in a balanced and sustainable approach to personal development.

7.8. Finding Fulfillment Beyond Work

Essentially, redefining identity and fulfillment outside of work roles is necessary to manage the emotional effects of redundancy. Even while losing a job is usually depressing, it may also be a strong catalyst for personal development, offering a chance to consider what really matters and investigate new possibilities for meaning and purpose. People can reestablish a sense of identity that is not exclusively connected to their jobs by using this opportunity to rediscover their beliefs, take up long-neglected hobbies, or partake in enjoyable activities. This more comprehensive viewpoint promotes emotional healing, resilience, and a basis for future achievement.

Exploring hobbies or passions that may have been neglected because of job obligations is sometimes the first step in redefining contentment. This time might be used, for example, to rekindle a past interest in writing, gardening, or photography. People might rediscover aspects of themselves that go beyond their professional identities through these artistic or leisure pursuits, which can provide them a sense of satisfaction and success. By providing a feeling of advancement and personal development at a period that may otherwise feel stagnant, taking up worthwhile hobbies or picking up new abilities can also help people feel more confident.

Another method to give back to the community and achieve fulfillment is via volunteering. Volunteering to help others creates a supporting network and relationships in addition to giving one a feeling of purpose. For instance, a previous executive may serve as a mentor to new professionals, imparting knowledge and assisting the upcoming generation of leaders. In a similar vein, someone with an educational degree may offer their time as a tutor, experiencing the inherent benefits of service while having a real influence. By fostering a sense of reciprocal value and appreciation, these efforts benefit the community as well as the person.

Redefining fulfillment may also be achieved by establishing new connections or strengthening current ones. Spending more time with loved ones or fostering connections that may have been neglected because of job obligations is frequently made possible by redundancy. Increasing these ties can help people feel more connected and emotionally supported, reminding them that their worth goes well beyond their position. In addition to enhancing both personal and professional life, networking with like-minded individuals in interest-based organizations or taking part in community events may open up new doors and views.

In addition to promoting emotional healing, meaningful activities offer direction and clarity for the future. These encounters frequently reveal latent abilities, fresh passions, or unrealized potential, which might lead to new business endeavors or career options. An artist who rekindles their love for painting, for example, may choose to sell their creations or provide art workshops, turning a hobby into a career. In a similar vein, someone who finds satisfaction in volunteering may choose to pursue a career in nonprofit or community service.

Overall, redundancy may be a catalyst for people to expand their sense of self and fulfillment, leading to a more fulfilling and well-rounded existence. Finding meaning and happiness outside of work can help people regain their self-esteem, heal emotionally, and face the future with more resilience and hope. In addition to enhancing wellbeing right away, these experiences set the stage for long-term success and fulfillment in both the personal and professional domains.

7.9. Conclusion: Navigating Emotional Recovery with Purpose

Managing the emotional fallout of redundancy is a complex but transformative process. By embracing acceptance, seeking support systems, and prioritizing self-care, individuals can navigate this challenging period with resilience and grace. These practices not only help alleviate immediate emotional distress but also foster personal growth and a renewed sense of purpose. Ultimately, redundancy is not just an ending—it can be the beginning of a journey toward greater self-awareness, strength, and fulfillment.

Chapter 8: Turning Job Loss into Opportunity

Although losing a job is undoubtedly difficult, it may also be a life-changing event that spurs development. Redundancy may seem like a setback at first, but it may also be a chance to take stock, think things through, and refocus one's personal and professional objectives. People can come out of this time with more clarity and purpose if they reframe losing their job as an opportunity to reevaluate goals, modify their current skill set, and try new things. This transitional period may result in the discovery of new possibilities and the creation of a more rewarding professional trajectory with deliberate personal evaluation, skill development, and focused initiatives.

Accepting the chance for introspection is the first step in using redundancy for progress. It is possible to assess previous jobs and experiences at this time of change, determining what worked and what didn't. Clarifying what really important may be achieved by asking questions like "What did I enjoy most about my previous job?" or "What values and priorities do I want my next role to reflect?" Reflection may indicate the need to move into a completely other field or position, the need for more work-life balance, or the pursuit of a passion that has previously been neglected. Setting deliberate, coordinated goals for their future actions is made possible by achieving this clarity.

Another crucial tactic during this period is to modify and enhance current abilities. The abilities that were useful in one profession may need to be broadened or updated to meet the demands of the present employment market, which is changing quickly. Redundancy presents an opportunity to pinpoint transferable talents, such technical proficiency, leadership, or problem-solving abilities, and investigate methods to improve them. To increase their employability, a person with experience in customer service, for example, may enroll in an online course in project management or digital communication. In a similar vein, professionals who wish to change careers should concentrate on earning credentials or training in pertinent fields to show that they are prepared for the change.

Creating a focused approach to your job search is just as crucial. Redundancy saves time, which enables a more proactive and thoughtful approach to identifying the next opportunity. This entails investigating fields, positions, and businesses that complement one's career and personal objectives. Job chances may be greatly improved by networking with specialists in the field, creating customized resumes and cover letters, and developing a strong LinkedIn presence. Participating in informational interviews, joining industry associations, or going to job fairs might also lead to opportunities that would not have otherwise been available. By keeping people motivated and focused, a well-defined plan transforms job seeking from a daunting undertaking into a purposeful, goal-driven activity.

Furthermore, redundancy might encourage people to pursue previously unconsidered entrepreneurial endeavors or alternate professional routes. For instance, a person who has always aspired to launch their own company or follow a creative interest could suddenly have the time and flexibility to make those goals a reality. These endeavors frequently provide a unique set of difficulties, but they can also result in incredibly fruitful and satisfying professional paths.

It's critical to keep a growth-oriented mentality during this process. People might approach the issue with interest and hope if they see redundancy as a temporary barrier rather than a permanent failing. Every action made, such as picking up a new skill, getting in touch with a mentor, or getting an interview, is a step closer to creating a more robust and resilient professional base.

Losing a job is undoubtedly challenging, but it also offers a special chance for reflection, development, and reinvention. Through careful job seeking, skill adaptation, and introspection, people may make the most of this transitional period to find new opportunities and build a rewarding, future-oriented professional path. Redundancy may be a springboard to more success and fulfillment if one is determined and has an open mind.

8.1. Reassessing Your Path: Discovering True Passions

Redundancy frequently compels people to take a step back and reconsider their professional trajectories. Sometimes a person's genuine passions and goals might be obscured by the everyday grind of employment. Losing a work offers a unique chance to consider what truly fulfills and fits with long-term objectives. After years in a corporate position, for example, a person may discover that they have a strong desire to work with nonprofits or launch their own company.

It is wise to approach this time of introspection with an open mind. Priorities and interests can be made clearer by journaling, consulting mentors, or even completing career assessment exams. Questions like "What kind of impact do I want to make?" and "What aspects of my previous job did I enjoy most?" can guide this exploration. Viewing redundancy as a pivot point, rather than a dead end, allows individuals to uncover paths they might not have considered otherwise.

8.2. Embracing Change as Growth

Fear of change is one of the many feelings that redundancy frequently causes. Because it forces people to confront new realities and leave their comfort zones, the uncertainty of what lies ahead can be frightening. Even though change can be frightening, it can also be a tremendous motivator for both professional and personal development. People who approach this change with an optimistic and receptive attitude might find new chances and create a more rewarding future. Redundancy is redefined when it is seen as an opportunity to develop rather than a setback, giving people the ability to take control of their own destiny.

Change can act as a catalyst for reassessing objectives and discovering unrealized possibilities. Someone laid off from a dwindling business, like retail or traditional manufacturing, for example, could take advantage of the chance to switch to a new field, like digital marketing, healthcare technology, or renewable energy. In addition to providing room for advancement, these professions also give chances to pick up new skills and match one's work to changing consumer needs. People may now view redundancy as a stepping stone rather than an end goal thanks to this reframing, which moves the emphasis from loss to opportunity.

Adopting a growth-oriented mentality is the first step towards accepting change. People might concentrate on what can be achieved rather than what has been lost. People are inspired to ask themselves questions such, "What industries excite me?" by this viewpoint, which promotes inquiry and discovery. or "How can I improve my skills to remain competitive in today's job market?" For instance, a logistics specialist may find that supply chain management in the quickly expanding field of e-commerce piques their interest and choose to obtain the necessary qualifications or training.

Additionally, resilience is fostered by a positive outlook, which aids people in overcoming the unavoidable difficulties that accompany change. Redefining redundancy as a normal aspect of one's career path helps to lessen the stigma associated with it and motivates action. Fear of failure is a typical obstacle. By offering direction and encouragement, friends, mentors, or career coaches may help make the process seem less intimidating.

It's often necessary to be proactive in order to explore novel possibilities. Attending workshops, taking online courses, or networking with experts in developing industries might lead to opportunities that were not previously thought about. To capitalize on the increasing demand for virtual education, an individual with an education background can, for example, look into chances in instructional design or online learning platforms. People who actively embrace change not only gain self-assurance but also broaden their perspectives.

In the end, seeing redundancy as an opportunity for development and reinvention turns what could otherwise seem like an insurmountable obstacle into a liberating one. People may rewrite their stories, choose new paths, and build a future full of possibilities when they embrace change with hope and resolve. Even if the path may be unpredictable, the benefits of development, education, and self-discovery make the change worthwhile.

8.3. Skill Realignment: The Power of Transferable Skills

Finding transferable skills—those adaptable qualities earned in prior employment that can be applied across sectors and professions—is one of the most useful and empowering things to do after losing a job. These abilities act as a bridge, enabling people to confidently move into other sectors or professional trajectories. By emphasizing these qualities, people may establish themselves as flexible, resourceful, and desirable applicants—even in positions or domains that might not appear familiar at first.

Transferable talents frequently fit into groups that are highly regarded in many different sectors. Strong communication abilities, for instance, are essential for positions in management, marketing, customer service, and education. Skills in project management, including team coordination, deadline management, and budgetary control, are highly valued across a variety of sectors, including technology, healthcare, and construction. For administrative and senior positions throughout industries, leadership abilities—which include inspiring colleagues, formulating strategic plans, and handling conflict—are highly sought for.

8.4. Skill Realignment: Mapping Strengths to Market Needs

Assessing prior experiences and determining how those skills match the demands of the market now is known as skill realignment. This method starts with a careful examination of prior positions and duties, emphasizing activities and achievements that demonstrate fundamental abilities. For example, a salesman who has demonstrated success in relationship-building, negotiating, and surpassing goals may be able to obtain employment in business development, account management, or fundraising. Similar to this, a teacher with public speaking, lesson planning, and mentoring abilities may be able to move into corporate training and development roles or instructional design jobs in e-learning organizations.

Presenting transferable talents in a way that appeals to potential employers is essential to maximizing their use. Candidates may stand out by customizing their cover letters and resumes to highlight these talents, particularly when switching to a new field. For instance, candidates can describe their experiences in terms of accomplishments and abilities rather than enumerating specific job duties from a prior position. For instance, they could say that they "led a cross-functional team to deliver projects on time and under budget" or "developed and maintained client relationships, resulting in a 20% increase in annual sales."

8.5. Expanding Career Options Through Transferable Skills

Finding transferable talents also enables people to look at prospects they might not have previously thought about and broaden their employment options. For instance, an individual with event planning expertise, which entails budget management, vendor negotiating, and organizational abilities, may be able to move into corporate event coordinating or operations management positions. A professional with a background in journalism may use their writing, research, and narrative skills to transition into positions in public relations, content marketing, or brand planning.

Transferable talents can occasionally uncover latent interests or strengths that lead to whole new career paths. A retail manager with strong team leadership and customer engagement skills, for example, may find that positions in human resources or hotel management are a natural match. Recognizing these possibilities can be both empowering and motivating, reducing the barriers to entering unfamiliar industries.

8.5.1. Leveraging Transferable Skills to Build Confidence

Prioritizing transferable talents is not just a sensible tactic; it is also a sentimental one. Self-confidence and a sense of capacity are reinforced at what may otherwise be a terrifying period when one recognizes their current abilities and how they can be applied to new challenges. It helps people approach their job search with hope and purpose by changing the narrative from one of "starting over" to one of "building on a strong foundation."

In the end, the foundation of flexibility in the fast-paced labor market of today is transferable talents. People may make job transitions easier and increase their chances of success by evaluating prior experiences, matching them with present needs, and clearly conveying their worth to potential employers. This strategy not only lowers the obstacles to breaking into new industries, but it also presents applicants as adaptable, strong, and prepared to make a significant contribution in their next position.

8.5.2. Upskilling to Bridge Gaps

Although transferable talents offer a solid basis for career changes, certain adjustments can necessitate learning new skills to satisfy the demands of an evolving labor market. Upskilling has emerged as a crucial tactic for filling up knowledge gaps, improving employability, and maintaining competitiveness in the fast-paced workplace of today. People can seek specialized learning opportunities in fields that correspond with their job aspirations through easily accessible and reasonably priced platforms such as Coursera, LinkedIn Learning, and edX. These tools enable people to acquire in-demand skills, show initiative, and establish themselves as flexible applicants prepared to succeed in new positions.

Finding the precise skills and competencies needed for a particular profession or sector is frequently the first step in upskilling. For instance, a person moving from a traditional marketing function to a digital marketing one would concentrate on developing their skills in data analytics, social media advertising, or SEO (Search Engine Optimization). These abilities, which may be obtained through certification programs or short-term online courses, are becoming more and more important in the marketing industry. In a similar vein, a project manager hoping to enter the computer sector may work for certifications in Scrum, Agile approaches, or software-specific technologies like Jira. These certifications match their profile with industry norms and improve their technical proficiency.

Upskilling has been transformed by the availability of online learning platforms, which enable people to learn from the comfort of their homes and at their own speed. While LinkedIn Learning offers industry-specific lessons intended for real-world application, platforms such as Coursera and edX provide courses from esteemed colleges and institutes. By providing free or inexpensive choices, many of these platforms lower the price barrier to education. Furthermore, both online and in-person courses and boot camps offer rigorous, practical instruction in fields like financial analysis, graphic design, and coding, enabling people to rapidly acquire and use new abilities.

In addition to bridging knowledge gaps, upskilling shows prospective employers effort and a growth-oriented mentality. A résumé or LinkedIn profile that highlights recently obtained certificates or abilities conveys a proactive dedication to both professional and personal growth. A professional who cites a recent certification in Google Analytics or Python programming, for example, not only demonstrates their technical prowess but also their dedication to keeping up with industry developments. In highly competitive employment markets, especially in industries experiencing fast innovation or change, this degree of initiative might help candidates stand out.

Adaptability is becoming more and more valued by employers, and upskilling is a concrete way to demonstrate this trait. Candidates demonstrate their readiness to take on difficulties and change with the industry by actively acquiring new skills. Organizations looking for workers who can contribute to innovation and handle the complexity of contemporary business settings will find this flexibility especially appealing.

Upskilling not only improves employability but also gives them a sense of confidence and empowerment. Acquiring new skills strengthens the conviction that, despite its difficulties, change may present a chance for development and reimagining. It changes the narrative from one of feeling unprepared to one of feeling competent and ready to thrive in a new position or sector.

In the end, upskilling is an investment in one's future that yields benefits for both career and personal development. People may demonstrate their worth to future employers, gain the skills necessary to succeed in a changing labor market, and make significant progress toward their professional objectives by utilizing online courses, certifications, and seminars. In addition to improving employability right away, this proactive strategy increases resilience for handling obstacles and changes in the future.

8.6. Strategic Job Hunting: Crafting a Winning Resume

The next important stage is to approach job seeking with a clear plan, beginning with creating a polished and focused résumé, after reevaluating professional goals and realigning abilities. A resume is an essential tool for getting interviews and moving forward in the recruiting process since it is the initial point of contact with potential employers. Candidates may show themselves as strong, determined, and very competent applicants by customizing this document to highlight pertinent experience, accomplishments, and transferable talents.

Customizing a CV for every job application is one of the best strategies to make it stand out. Employers are frequently turned off by generic resumes that detail every position and duty held in the past. Rather, applicants must to review the job description and determine the essential credentials, abilities, and experiences that the company is looking for. These ought to be prominently displayed on the resume, especially in areas such as the job history, abilities list, and professional description.

Particularly powerful are measurable accomplishments as they offer verifiable proof of a candidate's competence and efforts. Accomplishments are made concrete and memorable with statements like "increased sales by 30% in Q4," "streamlined operations to reduce processing time by 15%," or "managed a cross-functional team of 10 to complete projects ahead of schedule." Employers can more easily see how valuable a candidate may be to the company thanks to these measures, which show the breadth of prior duties as well as the quantifiable results of their work.

In the current employment environment, a lot of companies analyze resumes using applicant tracking systems (ATS) before sending them to a human reviewer. Candidates must include pertinent keywords from the job description in order to pass these systems. For instance, if a job posting highlights abilities like "project planning," "data analysis," or "customer relationship management," these phrases ought to flow organically from the CV. The probability that a resume will pass the first screening stage is increased when keywords are included exactly as they are in the skills and experience sections.

Another crucial place for personalization is the resume's summary section. This succinct introduction should highlight the candidate's most pertinent skills and goals while also closely matching the objectives of the company. For example, a marketing expert may write: "Six+ years of experience in digital strategy, content creation, and campaign optimization; results-driven marketing specialist." demonstrated ability to raise brand engagement by 40% attempting to use experience to propel creative marketing at [business name]. In addition to drawing readers in, a well-crafted synopsis establishes the tone for the whole work.

Action verbs are yet another essential component of a strong CV. Words like "led," "designed," "achieved," "implemented," and "streamlined" add energy and interest to descriptions while expressing confidence and initiative. For instance, applicants might state that they "managed and delivered multiple high-priority projects, ensuring timely completion and adherence to budget constraints" in place of "responsible for managing projects." This strategy not only shows the candidate's function but also their capacity for success.

Making a good impression also involves formatting and design. The resume will be simple to read and visually appealing if it has a neat, professional layout with consistent font choices, suitable space, and well defined parts. While section titles such as "Education," "Skills," and "Professional Experience" direct the reader through the page, bullet points should be utilized to highlight important facts and split up content.

Including each of these components on a resume shows professionalism, attention to detail, and a dedication to fulfilling the demands of potential employers. Candidates may greatly increase their chances of getting interviews and advancing toward their career objectives by customizing the document for each application, emphasizing measurable accomplishments, and optimizing for ATS compatibility. A methodical approach to resume writing guarantees that this crucial document functions as a potent marketing tool that distinguishes applicants in a crowded job market, in addition to being a record of prior experiences.

8.6.1. Optimizing Your LinkedIn Profile

A professional LinkedIn page is just as important for job searchers in the current digital era as a well-written CV. The platform is a vital tool in any smart job-hunting endeavor as recruiters and employers often utilize it to assess applicants and find possible hiring. In addition to showcasing credentials, a well-written LinkedIn profile acts as a dynamic representation of a person's personal brand, showcasing their accomplishments, experience, and career goals in an approachable and captivating manner.

Since a professional headshot is frequently the first thing recruiters see, it is the first step in creating a successful LinkedIn profile. One may make a good first impression with a crisp, high-quality photo, the right clothes, and a warm yet professional image. Photos are a crucial component of visibility and trustworthiness since they increase the likelihood that a profile will be seen compared to those without.

Another important element is the headline, which appears immediately under the profile name. The headline should be interesting and educational, emphasizing important abilities, positions, or industry emphasis, rather than just stating a current work title. For example, a headline can include "Digital Marketing Strategist | Specializing in SEO, Content Creation, and Campaign Optimization" rather than "Marketing Manager." This method lets prospective employers or partners know about your areas of expertise and value right away.

You have the chance to provide a personal and professional narrative in the summary area. A well-written summary should highlight a person's professional path, significant achievements, and future goals in a succinct yet powerful manner. For instance: "As a results-driven marketing specialist with more than 7 years of expertise in brand development and digital strategy, I am enthusiastic about spearheading successful campaigns that engage audiences with brands." I have experience in cross-functional team leadership, data-driven decision-making, and SEO. I'm now looking for chances to develop and create in the ever-evolving world of digital marketing. Adding pertinent keywords to this area also aids in LinkedIn's search engine optimization (SEO), making the profile more visible to recruiters looking for applicants with certain qualifications.

Beyond static profile elements, engagement with the platform is vital for building a professional presence. Regularly sharing industry insights, commenting on posts, or participating in discussions within LinkedIn groups demonstrates expertise and keeps the profile active in the eyes of connections. Posting original content, such as articles, thought leadership pieces, or reflections on industry trends, further enhances credibility and positions the individual as a knowledgeable and engaged professional.

Another essential component of LinkedIn's usefulness is networking. Making connections with peers, previous coworkers, managers, and business executives broadens one's professional network and opens doors to new possibilities and cooperation. Customized connection requests, such bringing up common interests or experiences, can add significance to outreach and boost acceptance rates.

Credibility is often increased by recommendations and endorsements from previous coworkers, managers, or partners. While written recommendations offer qualitative insights into work ethic, accomplishments, and professional manner, endorsements verify certain talents mentioned in the profile. A recommendation that emphasizes leadership in a high-pressure project or creativity in resolving challenging issues, for instance, may make a lasting impression on potential employers. Professional connections are strengthened and goodwill is fostered when suggestions are actively sought and reciprocated.

A strong LinkedIn profile is beneficial for long-term professional growth in addition to being a tool for job searches. Professionals may increase their exposure, show off their knowledge, and establish connections with a larger audience by fusing powerful visual components, engaging written material, and active platform involvement. In today's increasingly digital recruiting environment, job seekers are certain to stay competitive and well-positioned thanks to this strategic use of LinkedIn.

A professional LinkedIn page is just as crucial as a resume in the current digital era. The platform is an essential tool for strategic job seeking as recruiters and employers frequently use it to assess applicants. A professional headshot, an attention-grabbing headline, and a well-written text that highlights essential abilities and career goals are all components of a successful LinkedIn profile.

Using the platform on a regular basis to engage with peers, share industry ideas, and take part in conversations may boost exposure and show competence. Credibility is increased by recommendations and endorsements from previous superiors or coworkers, which further authenticate abilities and expertise.

8.6.2. Personalized Job Applications: Quality Over Quantity

The temptation to submit a large number of general applications when looking for a new position might be overwhelming. Personalized programs made for certain professions, however, work far better. Investigating the business, learning about its principles and objectives, then applying this information to cover letters and resumes demonstrates sincere interest and work. An applicant can stand out by, for instance, mentioning the company's recent accomplishments or tying personal objectives to its mission in a cover letter. Preparing well-thought-out applications shows professionalism and improves your chances of getting an interview.

8.6.3. Networking for Opportunities

Applying online is only one aspect of strategic job seeking; another is reaching out to professional networks. Referrals fill a lot of employment vacancies, therefore networking is an effective strategy. Undiscovered possibilities may arise via contacting old coworkers, going to industry events, and joining professional groups. LinkedIn and other social media sites are very useful for networking. Relationships that might result in employment offers can be developed by interacting with specialists in the field and sending tailored connection requests. Additionally, networking offers insightful information about possible career routes and industry trends.

8.6.4. Rebuilding Confidence During the Job Search

Self-confidence can often be undermined by job loss, leaving people uncertain of their skills and intimidated by the idea of reentering the workforce. Not only is it advantageous to rebuild self-esteem at this time, but it is also necessary to approach the search process with resilience and hope. Effective self-presentation to prospective employers requires confidence, and proactively regaining it may make the process easier and more rewarding.

One of the most effective ways to reaffirm progress and restore a sense of accomplishment is to celebrate little successes. Whether it's finishing an online course, revising a CV, or landing an interview, these accomplishments act as concrete reminders of one's strength and resolve. No matter how little these achievements may appear, recognizing and celebrating them helps to change the perspective from what has been lost to what is being gained, which promotes optimism.

Rebuilding confidence also requires practicing interview techniques. Many people have interview anxiety, particularly following a spell of unemployment. Whether conducted with a professional counselor, mentor, or close friend, mock interviews offer a secure setting for honing answers, addressing any shortcomings, and receiving helpful criticism. Anxiety may be considerably decreased by being familiar with typical interview questions and rehearsing well-considered, succinct responses. Additionally, concentrating on confident gestures, sitting up straight, and keeping eye contact are all examples of excellent body language that may assist project confidence in real interviews.

Maintaining a sense of balance and contentment requires equally significant personal development activities outside of the workplace. Engaging in volunteer work, community service, or hobby pursuits offers chances to rediscover interests, learn new skills, and make new friends. Participating in local sports, painting, or working at a nonprofit, for instance, not only enhances life but also acts as a reminder that one's worth goes well beyond their career. These pursuits can also serve as topics of discussion during interviews, demonstrating a proactive approach and a well-rounded personality.

In particular, volunteering provides the advantages of skill development and personal fulfillment. In addition to offering opportunities to develop or exhibit transferable talents, helping a cause one cares about promotes a feeling of purpose and connection. For example, planning a community event might demonstrate leadership and project management skills, while mentoring others demonstrates interpersonal and communication skills.

Last but not least, putting an emphasis on mental and physical health builds resilience and confidence. Frequent exercise, mindfulness exercises, and upholding a healthy routine boost energy and mood, enabling people to face obstacles with greater clarity and optimism. People may approach the job hunt with newfound drive when they take little measures like these, which help to create a comprehensive feeling of preparation.

8.7. Conclusion: Turning Setbacks into Stepping Stones

It takes initiative and planning to turn losing a job into an opportunity. People may turn redundancy into a springboard for a more rewarding career by reevaluating their professional objectives, matching their talents to market demands, and employing focused job-hunting techniques. Even if the path might be difficult, it offers the opportunity for personal development, rebirth, and self-discovery. Losing a job may become a fresh start full of possibilities and promise if you are persistent, flexible, and have a well-defined strategy.

Chapter 9: Living a Fulfilled Life Despite Uncertainty

The concept of leading a meaningful life might seem elusive in a society that is becoming more and more defined by rapid mutations and unforeseen difficulties. Uncertainty brought on by personal failures, career changes, and economic ups and downs frequently makes it hard to concentrate on what really important. But outward stability is not always a prerequisite for contentment. Even in the midst of uncertainty, people may create a full and fulfilling life by redefining success, cultivating appreciation, and engaging in important hobbies.

9.1. Redefining Success: Moving Beyond Job Titles

Many people have historically defined success in terms of material belongings, pay, or job titles. Although these successes might be satisfying, they frequently don't result in long-term fulfillment. Individuals may concentrate on what really matters—realizing their potential, changing the world, and building lasting relationships—by redefining success as a path of personal development and service.

For instance, someone facing job uncertainty might shift their focus from climbing the corporate ladder to enhancing their skills or mentoring others. This perspective not only alleviates the pressure to achieve conventional milestones but also fosters a sense of purpose and self-worth. By prioritizing personal values over societal expectations, individuals can create a more authentic and fulfilling definition of success.

In uncertain times, redefining success also involves focusing on what is within your control. External circumstances, such as market conditions or organizational changes, may be unpredictable, but personal growth and contribution are always achievable. For example, learning a new skill, supporting a friend in need, or improving physical and mental health are areas where individuals can make tangible progress, regardless of external challenges.

In addition to fostering resilience, this strategy supports the notion that success extends beyond one's career. It serves as a reminder to people that living in accordance with their principles and having a good influence on both their own and other people's lives is the path to fulfillment.

9.2. Practicing Gratitude: The Power of the Present Moment

Gratitude is a powerful tool for cultivating contentment, even during uncertain times. People may shift from a mindset of scarcity to one of plenty by focusing on life's positive aspects and celebrating little achievements. Gratitude makes individuals feel happier and less worried about the future by keeping their attention on the present. For example, one may think of the support of family, the joy of one's own hobbies, or the opportunity to explore new chances instead of dwelling on professional setbacks. This mindset may be reinforced and used as a tangible reminder of life's blessings by keeping a gratitude notebook, where one writes down three things each day for which they are thankful.

9.3. Pursuing Interests: Enriching Life Through Passion

Hobbies, volunteer work, and community service are important sources of balance and enjoyment, particularly in difficult times. Aside from providing a stress release, engaging in hobbies outside of work also promotes happiness and a sense of achievement. In addition to providing useful time, hobbies like playing an instrument, caring for a garden, or playing sports in the community encourage creativity and personal development. These activities provide a mental reset that enables people to put aside the stresses of uncertainty and concentrate on something they truly like.

Another advantage of hobbies is that they may help people meet people who have similar interests. For instance, taking part in group hikes or joining a photography club offers a chance to network, meet new people, and form relationships. These kinds of relationships, which foster a feeling of community and provide emotional support, can be particularly significant during trying times. Additionally, hobbies enable people to discover new facets of themselves, frequently revealing latent abilities or passions that might result in unanticipated chances for growth on both a personal and professional level.

Volunteering takes the idea of engagement a step further by providing a way to give back to the community while finding purpose. Activities such as mentoring students, organizing local events, or supporting charitable causes not only contribute to the greater good but also help individuals develop a sense of belonging and self-worth. For instance, someone experiencing job loss might find solace in helping others navigate similar challenges through career coaching or volunteering at a local unemployment resource center. This act of giving back can be deeply empowering, reminding individuals that their skills and experiences have value beyond traditional professional settings.

Additionally, volunteering frequently provides access to fresh viewpoints and possibilities. Working with several organizations or causes exposes people to a variety of viewpoints and can spur personal development and change. Volunteering at a food bank or environmental project, for instance, may inspire a renewed interest in social or ecological campaigning, which may have an impact on future professional decisions or lifestyle adjustments. In the end, making time for worthwhile endeavors, whether via volunteer work, hobbies, or community service, improves life, fosters resilience, and enables people to keep a feeling of connection and purpose even in the face of adversity.

9.4. Building Connections Through Community Engagement

One of the most effective ways to improve one's life, make relationships, and create useful social networks is through community participation. People can meet like-minded persons, exchange experiences, and build enduring relationships by joining local groups, taking part in group activities, or attending courses. These relationships frequently result in new friendships, teamwork, and even unanticipated chances that may greatly improve one's personal and professional life. Interacting with others in a common area fosters a feeling of community and support, which is particularly beneficial in uncertain or transitional times

For example, a person who enjoys writing might join a local writers' group, where they can share their work, receive constructive feedback, and learn from others. Through regular interaction with peers, they not only improve their craft but also develop friendships with people who share their passion for storytelling. Over time, these relationships could evolve into collaborative projects, such as co-authoring a book or organizing a community literary event, showcasing how community engagement can lead to meaningful creative opportunities.

Those who are passionate about protecting the environment might find satisfaction by taking part in ecological cleanup events or sustainability projects. One practical method to support environmental preservation is to participate in a local beach clean-up organization or tree-planting initiative. These activities provide people a feeling of pride and purpose in helping a worldwide problem in addition to connecting them with like-minded others. Additionally, these activities might spark new interests or abilities. For example, a volunteer for a recycling awareness campaign may find they have a talent for lobbying or public speaking, which could lead to additional involvement or perhaps employment chances in the industry.

Additionally, workshops and skill-sharing gatherings provide unique opportunities for interpersonal growth and community engagement. For example, taking a pottery class or culinary workshop may be a worthwhile opportunity to meet others who share your interests and learn a new skill. Participants frequently create groups that meet periodically to discuss progress or work together on projects, demonstrating how these relationships go beyond the actual activity. In addition to improving social well-being, these relationships build a network of people who promote one another's growth. In each instance, community involvement turns personal passions into group achievements and acts as a link to deeper, more connected lives.

9.5. The Role of Mindset in Fulfillment

In spite of uncertainty, a growth-oriented mentality is essential for achieving contentment. When people see obstacles as chances for growth and self-discovery, they may overcome them with fortitude and optimism. For example, one may regard uncertainty as an opportunity to improve relationships, learn new skills, or explore new opportunities rather than as a danger. This change in perspective promotes a feeling of empowerment and strengthens the conviction that internal strength and flexibility, rather than steadiness from the outside, are what lead to fulfillment. It inspires people to confidently and curiously accept life's unpredictable nature.

Uncertainty frequently inspires introspection and offers a chance to reevaluate goals and values. Finding a feeling of direction and purpose can be facilitated by posing queries like "What really matters to me?" and "How can I make a positive impact?" In addition to directing choices, this introspection enhances life by bringing behaviors into line with goals and ideals. When values and actions are in harmony, a sense of fulfillment is created. For example, a person who values creativity might use a career change to pursue artistic endeavors or entrepreneurial endeavors, while a person who values connection might place more importance on forming relationships or supporting community projects.

9.6. Thriving Despite Uncertainty

It takes deliberate effort and a change in viewpoint to lead a fulfilled life in the face of uncertainty. People may discover happiness and purpose in the present moment by reframing achievement, cultivating appreciation, and engaging in important hobbies. Regardless of external factors, these activities build resilience, enhance day-to-day living, and lay the groundwork for personal growth and fulfilment. In the end, finding contentment involves accepting life's possibilities and challenges with an open mind and heart, not eradicating uncertainty.

9.7. Conclusion

It is a difficult experience to navigate uncertainty, particularly when it comes to career transitions and job stability. But it also presents opportunities for development, self-awareness, and fortitude. People may turn times of transition into stepping stones toward a better future by adopting tactics like creating emergency money and managing debt, redefining success beyond job titles, and finding meaningful hobbies outside of work. In addition to easing the immediate stressors of job loss or uncertainty, these resources help people develop a feeling of purpose and empowerment that goes well beyond the office.

The key to thriving in the face of uncertainty is mindset and actions. Emotional rehabilitation begins with accepting oneself and dealing with the emotional consequences of redundancy without passing judgment. The connection and support required to overcome obstacles may be found in asking friends, family, or experts for help, and self-care restores vitality and affirms one's value. It is impossible to overestimate the value of being thankful and acknowledging our little victories because they keep us rooted in the here and now, serve as a reminder of life's good things, and strengthen our resolve for the future.

Career changes should be seen as a continuation of a larger journey rather than as its conclusion. Every step is an opportunity to develop and discover new opportunities, whether it's reevaluating one's career path, realigning skills, or starting a strategic job search. Change and redundancy may seem like setbacks at first, but they may also be opportunities to explore interests, develop talents, and find passions that lead to a more balanced and satisfying existence. By utilizing resources like well-crafted resumes, networking, and ongoing education, people may confidently traverse the changing labor market.

The strength of resilience is at the core of prospering in the face of uncertainty. Resilient people can adjust to difficulties, welcome change, and never give up on their objectives. It is the inner strength that serves as a reminder that our distinctive abilities, beliefs, and interests are what truly make us valuable, not a job title. Building resilience enables people to reinterpret who they are outside of their work responsibilities and live authentically and purposefully.

Though it may take unexpected twists, the path to fulfillment is also enhanced by the chances for connection and personal development that come with adjusting to change. People may not only get over their worries of redundancy but also flourish in the midst of uncertainty by utilizing their abilities, taking part in worthwhile activities, and keeping a proactive mentality. The strategies covered—financial readiness, emotional fortitude, strategic planning, and community involvement—provide a road map for leading a happy and meaningful life, independent of outside events.

The difficulties of career transitions and job security pressures are ultimately universal, but they do not characterize us. We can face uncertainty with courage and thrive by creating a life based on our inner resilience, passions, and strengths because of our ability to adapt, grow, and create meaning. For those who choose to embrace the journey with hope and determination, the future is full of possibilities despite its unpredictability.

This book provides a compassionate yet realistic approach to assist readers in overcoming job insecurity, overcoming fears of redundancy, and creating a stable and satisfying life.

www.ingramcontent.com/pod-product-compliance
Lightning Source LLC
Chambersburg PA
CBHW052203220526
45471CB00004B/1794